Spitballs in the Night

MEMORIES OF MY YEARS
IN A CHILDREN'S HOME

CORINNE BRISCOE ELLIOTT

Edited by
Anna Elliott Utick

Illustrations by
Neva Sebert Wallace

"Spitballs In The Night"
Copyright © 1998 Corinne Briscoe Elliott
Copyright © 2011 Lotus Light Publishing, LLC

Editor's Notes:
Acknowledgments, Foreword, Introduction,
About the Author, Afterword, Back Cover Text
Copyright © 2011 Anna Elliott Utick

Illustrations
Copyright © 2011 Neva Sebert Wallace

Cover
Copyright © 2011 Lotus Light Publishing, LLC

All rights reserved.
ISBN-10: 061551975X
ISBN-13: 978-0615519753

No part of this publication may be reproduced in any form
or by any means without the prior written permission
of the Publisher or Editor, except by a reviewer,
who may quote brief passages for a review.

Lotus Light Publishing, LLC
1526 Stuart Street
Helena, MT 59601-2332

DEDICATION

Lovingly dedicated to Fern Bixel
and to Margaret May Brooks.

CONTENTS

	Acknowledgments	i
	Foreword	ii
	Introduction	iv
1	It's Not a Summer Camp, My Dear	1
2	Cold Cream and Hanky Rags	5
3	Rosie the Riveting	12
4	Pockets	15
5	Got Hot Rocks	20
6	New Digs	25
7	One Big Blister	29
8	New Delights	33
9	"The Lone Ranger," In a Nutshell	39
10	Sew a Fine Seam	45
11	Sweet Valentines	48
12	The All-Night Easter Bunny	51
13	It's All In Your Head	54
14	The Chocolate Burial	58
15	A Playmate's Departure	62
16	Twilight's Last Gleaming	68
17	New Friendships	72
18	More Than Music Lessons	75
19	More Lessons and Howls	80
20	Let's Run Away	84
21	Again, It's All In Your Head	87
22	Immortal Youth	90
23	Greener Grass	94
24	Before Training Bras	99
25	Aggie's Mom	102
26	All That Soap	107
27	Greta Keeps a Secret	111
28	Changes For Miss Fern's Charges	114
29	Miss Fern's Announcement	118
	Poem, "Founded on Love"	124
	Epilogue	125
	About the Author	127
	Afterword	128

ACKNOWLEDGMENTS

Many special thanks to Neva Sebert Wallace for her wonderful illustrations and general, overall help with the project. Great appreciation also goes to the Editor's husband, Andy Utick, for his help in the various processes involved in bringing the manuscript to publication.

– Anna Elliott Utick

FOREWORD

Corinne Briscoe Elliott always wished to share these memories in book form, but passed away before that dream came to fruition. Thus, the publication effort was undertaken by her daughter and son-in-law, Anna Elliott Utick and Andrew J. Utick; with considerable help also from her cousin, Neva Sebert Wallace, who provided the illustrations.

Although all the stories in this book are true reminiscences of the author's years at the Methodist Deaconess Orphanage in Lake Bluff, Illinois (later known as the Lake Bluff Children's Home), she assigned fictional names to the characters, for obvious reasons.

We believe that it was the author's desire that these stories might help to change the somewhat negative opinions held by many regarding orphanages, in general. Even though the place was named as an orphanage during the decade or so that she was there, she always insisted that it be referred to as a "children's home," not an "orphanage." She treasured her memories of those years and maintained the many friendships formed during that time, all of which truly enriched her life.

– Anna Elliott Utick

HONEYSUCKLE
(Lonicera sp.)

INTRODUCTION

Corinne Briscoe was born in Chicago in 1927, the second of four daughters, and was left as the eldest when her older sister died at the age of four years in 1929. Aside from this very sad event, her early family life was pleasant, leaving her with many happy memories. However, when she was about six or seven, her parents became very ill and unable to care for her and her sisters, so the children were sent to live with their paternal grandmother, a widow who ran a boarding house in Chicago. Corinne's two younger sisters, who were five and seven years her junior, were too young to actually help with the cleaning and other chores at the boarding house, so they went to the Lake Bluff Children's Home, then known as the Methodist Deaconess Orphanage, in April of 1938. In about 1939, Corinne was sent to the MDO, as well.

Once having been placed at the Methodist Deaconess Orphanage, the sisters never again saw their mother alive, and saw their father only once. Their grandmother corresponded with them and occasionally visited them, when she could get away from her boarding house responsibilities. The girls, in turn, were occasionally able to visit their grandmother by traveling to Chicago by train. Corinne saw her father again shortly before her marriage in 1947. He was ill with tuberculosis and was residing at his mother's boarding house at that time.

Corinne and her two sisters were in different buildings at the children's home: Corinne, in Judson Hall; the middle sister, in Swift Hall; and the youngest, in the "babyfold." Because of the residential age separation at the MDO and the various scheduled routines, Corinne did not spend a great deal of time with her younger sisters during her years there.

Through her high school years, Corinne was fostered out to a few families. The first one was not wonderful, and she was treated more like an indentured servant. She was then placed with another family, staying in their son's room while he was away in military training. The mother in that family was a music teacher, and had a strong influence on Corinne's love of music. Corinne left when the son returned, and was then placed with another family, who regarded her as one of their own.

Although several of Corinne's foster families, as well as one of the matrons at the children's home, expressed interest in adopting her, this was not possible because her father would not sign over his parental rights, a necessary first step to the adoption process.

Corinne's official association with the children's home came to an end when she married William S. Elliott, just a week after graduating from Lake Forest High School, in 1947. The happy couple moved to his native state of Montana and lived the rest of their lives there, but Corinne always stayed in touch with those with whom she'd formed deep bonds of friendship during her years at the institution that was later named the Lake Bluff Children's Home.

For Corinne, the adage, "Home is where the heart is," was absolutely true. She considered the children's home at

Lake Bluff to be her main childhood home, and realized full well that it was the best option for her during those years. She regarded her foster families as her own, and stayed in touch with them throughout her life, until they passed on, many decades later. Above all, she felt extremely fortunate to have lived at the place that was later renamed as the Lake Bluff Children's Home, and always treasured her memories of those years.

1 – IT'S NOT A SUMMER CAMP, MY DEAR

Agatha Broward pressed her nose against the train window and stared at the sooty brick buildings as the train passed by the backyards of the city. She imagined that the train was standing still and the buildings were moving past her view. The wooden staircases that zigzagged up the backs of the buildings reminded her of splintered zippers. She bounced gently on the green velvet seat as she thought about the fun she would have at summer camp. The prospect of summer camp to Agatha meant new friends, swimming, snacks, campfire stories, and great meals. The clickety-clack of the train's wheels reminded her of the rhythm in a song as she traveled farther away from her grandmother's home. But she would be back. After all, her grandmother had told her she was going to summer camp.

She gazed out the window and noticed that the train had

carried her past the blackened brick and wood buildings of the city to quiet towns with tree-lined streets graced by attractive homes. The lady taking her to summer camp dozed lightly in a seat across the aisle. She looked peaceful with her head resting against the window sash. Aggie liked Miss Wood, a cheerful lady with rimless glasses and gray hair attractively pulled into an ample bun at the back of her head. There was something solid and dependable about her, in Agatha's opinion. She knew because, whenever Miss Wood visited Agatha's grandmother, she smiled a lot and spoke with a quiet confidence that Agatha had not seen, even in the teachers at school. Of course, the teachers were tired, she mused; a new school was under construction in their neighborhood, so classes were held in empty stores. Sometimes, Agatha had to share her desk because the classes were crowded. The teachers hardly ever smiled, and sometimes they were downright cranky. Miss Wood was different, and Agatha liked the difference.

Soon, Miss Wood stirred, blinked her eyes, and looked out the window as though checking progress on their trip. She smiled at Agatha, and then opened her purse, pulled out a pretty hanky with lace around the edge, and cleaned her glasses. After that, she smoothed her hair, put her glasses on, and smiled at Agatha again.

"Are you enjoying the train ride?" Miss Wood asked.

"OOOOOH, YES!" Agatha responded. "And I can hardly wait to get to summer camp!"

Miss Wood's face changed. Agatha could not tell whether she was about to cry or was a little ticked off. Her mouth looked grim. She seemed to study her lap. Meanwhile Agatha twirled her straight, blonde hair with an index finger. She shifted in her seat and smoothed her blue and white striped dress over her knees. Then Miss Wood spoke.

"Agatha, why do you think you are going to summer camp?"

"Grandma told me." She paused while the pit of her stomach adjusted itself. "I am going to summer camp, aren't I?"

"My dear, it's not a summer camp. It's an orphanage."

Miss Wood turned her head away and stared out the window.

Agatha felt as though she had just fallen through a trap door. She felt betrayed. What was it her dad used to say – "shanghaied." He explained the word to her one time when they were drawing cartoons and telling jokes to each other. *Poor Dad. So sick.*

Why did Grandma tell me it was a summer camp?

The word, "orphanage," reminded Agatha of Miss Meany and Annie Rooney from the Sunday "comics" – and Little Orphan Annie. And tall, pointed wrought iron fences. Shut off from the world. Agatha never heard of a good orphanage. And why was Grandma sending her away? Agatha thought about times when she was shopping with her mother, and she would hear parents threaten their children with, "If you're not good, I'm going to send you to an orphanage."

Well, I was good, she silently insisted. *Won't Grandma miss my help around that big house? Grandma has such a big house. And she's always vacuuming, dusting, or collecting rent from the roomers.* She decided that maybe Grandma was just tired. *But an orphanage!*

Agatha's stomach felt like a ball of lead. Suddenly, it seemed to her that the train wheels no longer played a tune.

Instead, they seemed to howl. Like a sick animal. She looked across the aisle at Miss Wood. Her face was still turned away. And her eyes were still closed.

Agatha felt such a lump in her throat, she was afraid it would shut off her breathing; but she closed her eyes and swallowed. After all, big nine-year-old girls don't cry -- at least, not very often or in public. She wished she was with her dad and mom. She thought about how pale her mom had looked last time she saw her. Her mom had coughed a lot.

The train was slowing down for another town. *How many towns have we passed through?* Every time the train had passed through a station, Agatha had felt a sense of anticipation. But that was gone, now. In its place was a feeling of dread.

Miss Wood stirred as the conductor announced the town. She stood up and fished some packages off the overhead rack.

"This is where we get off," Miss Wood said. Agatha stood and smoothed her dress over her thin frame. She began to wonder what kind of impression she would make on her own version of Miss Meany. The train lurched to a stop and Agatha had to grab the back of the seat to keep from falling.

"Follow me," Miss Wood invited as she led the way down the train's aisle. They stepped off the train into a warm afternoon. But Aggie felt stiff and cold.

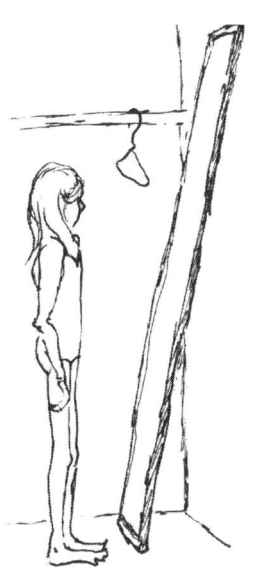

2 – COLD CREAM AND HANKY RAGS

The wooden boards of the train station felt warm through the soles of Agatha's patent leather shoes. The sun was wending its way west, and Agatha tried hard to loosen her tense muscles. Even her jaw felt clamped shut.

After adjusting her packages, Miss Wood offered her hand to Agatha. Together, they walked across a bridge toward the center of town. To Agatha, this quiet town was a contrast to the clanging streetcars, noisy elevated trains, the clop-clopping of horse-drawn milk wagons, and shrieking grocers at open air markets. A line of storefronts boasted a dry cleaner, library, small grocery, and a lawyer. Across another street, the sign on a modest brick building stated, "Ice Cream and News."

On they walked, down a sleepy street where the branches

of oak and maple trees reached across the sidewalks to each other.

Agatha could hear supper sounds through open doorways.

And suddenly, as they crossed a street to what Agatha thought was a college campus, Miss Wood squeezed Agatha's hand and said,

"Here we are." Miss Wood smiled down at her.

Agatha gazed in disbelief at the sweeping lawn shaded by a random collection of maple, oak, and shagbark hickory. Handsome brick buildings bordered the lawn. *No high iron fences,* Agatha marveled. *Anywhere. What kind of orphanage is this??*

A line of honeysuckle bushes began a long march down the block from where the rolling lawn ended. The town surrounded the institution, and seemed to make it part of the community. Agatha's jaw began to relax. She felt hungry.

Their first stop was at a building on the edge of the grounds to announce their arrival. Then they continued on to a building covered by Virginia creeper.

On the second floor, they walked down a wide hall and followed the sound of quiet voices and occasional laughter to a large room with round tables where girls about Agatha's age sat, eating sandwiches. A pleasant-looking lady sat with them. She looked up and smiled as Miss Wood led Agatha into the room.

"Miss Fern, I'd like for you to meet Agatha Broward. She's come to join your family." Miss Fern stood and took Agatha's hand.

"Welcome, Agatha! Come sit down and join us with something to eat. This is 'sandwich night.' Later on, we'll go down to the beach for a swim." Miss Fern reached for a basket and held it out to Agatha. Agatha realized how hungry she really was as she looked into an assortment of sandwiches, fruit, cookies, and milk as well as napkins and paper plates.

Well, this doesn't seem like an orphanage -- yet, thought Agatha as she loaded her plate while Miss Fern walked Miss Wood to the door and said goodbye. Agatha looked around at a variety of faces, some studying her, some smiling, some mischievous. One girl looked sullen and resentful. Agatha took a few bites, and then broke the silence:

"My friends call me Aggie." The girls stirred and Miss Fern nodded.

"Now, you know Aggie, girls. She wants to know who you are. Betty, why don't you start? And Shirley next, and so on."

"Sure. My name's Betty Ann."

"Shirley Marie. But just call me Shirley."

"Alice."

"Grace."

"Esther."

"Rose Marie. But everybody calls me Rosie."

"Pat."

"Annabelle. Ann for short."

"Beverly."

"Sally," the quiet, sullen girl whispered.

"That's all of us, Aggie. Claire is at the little children's home helping out tonight. She'll be back later." Miss Fern looked around the tables. "After everyone is finished, girls, put all your paper plates and napkins in the waste basket. Then we'll go put our swimsuits on. Aggie, do you have a swimsuit?"

"Not really, Miss Fern. I'm not sure if all my stuff arrived, either."

"We'll see what we have, then. A few extra suits are in the hall closet."

A horn of plenty, Aggie amended to herself. She noticed that most of the girls were finished eating, but didn't leave the table. Some talked to each other, some elbowed a neighbor and giggled, but all stayed. Aggie finished quickly. Esther stood.

"Miss Fern, may I be excused to take the basket back to the dining hall?"

"You may. It looks as though all the girls are finished. You may all be excused to go change. Aggie, come with me." Aggie followed Miss Fern down the hall to a door that opened to a walk-in closet. Miss Fern pulled a box from the shelf and brought out some bathing suits.

"Try these on," Miss Fern held out a few suits to Aggie. "You may change in the bathroom. I'll come with you and see which fits you best." They hurried down the hall to the bathroom and Aggie went into one of the stalls, shut the door, and kicked off her shoes. Her first try looked like a sunsuit. She decided to think about it. Then she tried on a very smart-looking navy blue suit with a SHAPE to it.

Wow! Do I dare wear such a glamour suit? What will I look like in this?! Aggie discovered that it even had a well-known label in it. She tried it on and stepped out of the stall. Miss Fern smiled. Just then, Claire came in. She looked at Aggie and then Miss Fern.

"Claire, this is our new girl, Aggie."

"Hi," Aggie ventured to a staring Claire.

"Miss Fern, why can't I have that suit, and Aggie have

mine? She's so flat, and I could fill that one out!"

"Why, your suit looks fine on you, Claire! You have a nice shape and you fill your suit out just right!" Miss Fern reminded Claire.

She certainly does have a shape, agreed Aggie, silently. *And I am sort of straight up and down. Skinny. But I love this swimsuit, and maybe its style will make up for my shapeless look.*

"I don't care! I should have that suit! It's so stylish!"

"Claire, go put on the suit you have. We're leaving for the lake soon!" Miss Fern closed the subject. Aggie took a hesitant look into the mirror to see if she should give up on wearing the pretty, one-piece suit. Her reflection revealed a skinny kid with a truly glamorous suit and a bra area that was empty but shapely, due to the style of the suit and the expertise of whomever had put it together.

"Well, I think that suit will be alright, Aggie. And don't worry. In a couple of years, you'll fill it out." Miss Fern nodded her approval. "Now let's all get going. By the time we get to the beach, it will have been an hour since we ate." Miss Fern left and called down the hallway, "Girls, remember your buddy tags!"

Betty Ann poked her head in the doorway and said,

"Aggie, will you be my buddy? I've got your tag here. Go ahead – pin it on."

Miss Fern walked behind the girls, and occasionally reminded them not to get too far ahead. Aggie noticed new, strange smells along the way: The late-afternoon spice of warm trees; the sweet, fragrant perfume of a vacant lot crowded with wild raspberry bushes; and the wet, mulchy smell of leaves covering the shaded ground on the bluff above the beach. Far different from the coal and kerosene smells of the city, mixed with the diesel fumes of buses as they hummed past the lumbering, clanking streetcars.

On the beach, lots of people, some with picnic baskets, already sat about visiting and playing in the sand while others bounded about in the waves of the lake. Aggie quickly kicked off her shoes and socks.

"Girls, gather 'round," Miss Fern ordered. Expectant faces looked up at her. "Remember the buddy system. Stay close to your buddy, and don't anyone stray too far from the rest of the group. Come back in when I blow the whistle. I'll be watching from right here," she patted a rock. Everyone raced to the water.

"Do you know the crawl?" Betty Ann inquired as soon as she caught up with Aggie.

"No, but I can dog-paddle."

"I'll show you." Betty did a few strokes and Aggie tried to imitate them. Much laughing, splashing, thrashing, and paddling almost drowned out the sound of the whistle. Time had gone by too fast. It was time to go back.

Bedtime came quickly. Miss Fern assigned a bed to Aggie in the same dorm room as Betty Ann, Esther, Pat, Rosie, and Claire. Aggie was tired and felt relieved to crawl between the cool, crisp sheets on her bed. Miss Fern came into the room and kissed each girl. Aggie noticed that she carried an industrial-size jar of cold cream and a hand full of square cloths.

"That's cold cream and hanky rags," Esther whispered from the next bed.

Miss Fern came to Aggie's bed. "Hold out your hand, Aggie, and I'll give you some cold cream." Aggie held out her hand while Miss Fern doled out a glob of the creamy stuff. "Now spread that on your face, neck and hands. Here's a hanky rag to dob up the excess," Miss Fern smiled as she bent to kiss Aggie goodnight. At the door, Miss Fern said "Goodnight," once more and left.

"Psssst! Aggie! Don't do anything yet! We'll show you what we really do with the cold cream and hanky rags," came a voice out of the growing darkness. Esther got out of bed and took the hanky rag from Aggie. She tore it into strips, tied the strips into knots, and dipped them into the cold cream.

"Now watch," whispered Esther. She tossed a knotted, cold-cream-drenched rag up to the ceiling over Claire's bed. The blob stuck to the ceiling. Aggie helped Esther tear the other hanky rag into strips, tie them into knots, and generously slather them in the cold cream. Soon, the ceiling was dotted with white knots of cloth, waiting for the proper time to drop on a sleeping girl. No one would be spared from the "spitballs in the night." Many giggles later, Aggie drifted off to sleep thinking to herself that Miss Fern was certainly no Miss Meany.

3 – ROSIE THE RIVETING

Rosie was round and loud – a rotund challenge to any new kid on the block – or in the dorm.

"Betcha yer 'fraid o' me!" Rosie boasted as she sashayed toward Aggie.

"No, I'm not!" Aggie retorted while thinking that Rosie must come from a big city, as she herself had. There were kids like Rosie in the neighborhoods where she had lived.

"Well, then! You skinny little runt, why don't you fight with me?!"

"I don't like to fight!"

"Yer 'fraid I'll beat you up, cuz I'm bigger'n you are, ya little coward!"

"I'm not a coward! I just don't see why we have to fight!" The other girls began to gather around the two. While Rosie taunted Aggie, Esther whispered into Aggie's ear,

"She does this to all the new girls, and she'll pester you until you fight her."

Oh, crumb! thought Aggie, as deja vu closed in on her. She remembered being in a line on a school playground after lunch before the school doors opened to let the kids in for afternoon classes. A chocolate-brown girl in a pink dress and shiny black braids bore down on her and began to shriek at her. Aggie had never seen the girl before and didn't know what she was screaming about. Aggie tried to make out the run-together words in an accent different from her own. Finally, the girl ran out of words and sauntered away.

If only Rosie would just saunter away, Aggie silently prayed, just as Rosie closed in and gave Aggie a push. That raised the adrenalin in Aggie and she pushed back. Then Rosie pushed harder, but Aggie grabbed Rosie's arms in an effort to regain balance. Rosie tried to grab Aggie's hair, but Aggie had a tight grip on Rosie's arms and shifted slightly to get a better handhold; but somehow, Aggie scratched Rosie's arm in the effort, and Rosie let out a scream.

"I'm bleeding!" she yelled, and ran off, whimpering, to Miss Fern who boiled out of her sewing room and marched toward the cluster of girls.

"Aggie! Is it true that you scratched Rosie?"

"I didn't mean to, Miss Fern."

"It's un-Christian to fight! Don't you remember the Bible passage I read a few nights ago about turning the other cheek?"

"But, Miss Fern, I had to defend myself!"

"No more fighting, girls! Go outside and play!" Miss Fern closed the subject and took Rosie, sniffling, back to the sewing room to put merthiolate on her scratch.

"See? You won! Good for you!" Esther and the other girls affirmed what Aggie already suspected.

"C'mon! Let's get a softball game going!" Claire urged, and smiled at Aggie.

Gosh, if I'd turned the other cheek to Rosie, she'da knocked my block off! Aggie observed.

But Rosie never challenged Aggie again.

4 – POCKETS

"I'm so hungry I could eat a horse!" Betty caught up with Aggie on the way to the dining hall.

"I could eat two horses!" Aggie laughed. "I'm so glad you told me how to watch the ball when it's coming at me!"

"You're good now, Ag! You even hit a home run today!"

"It's more fun now! And good not to be the last one picked for sides!"

They entered the cool dining hall and found seats at their table. Aggie thought the dining hall looked attractive, with the long tables and a few round ones, all covered with heavy white tablecloths and with cloth napkins that stayed in place all week. Miss Fern took her place at the halfway point of the long table used by the girls on her floor. All the chatter ceased while someone stood and asked the blessing. Then all the chatter began again as the dining room workers from various dorms delivered bowls of the main course, salad, bread, and butter to the table.

Something was different this night. Where there was usually some kind of meat dish, tonight there was a vegetable salad in gelatin. There was also a fruit salad, along with the bread and butter. And a custard for dessert. To Aggie, the gelatin salad looked promising. But other girls had doubts.

"That gelatin has no color," Betty noted.

"It's not red, or green, or purple," Grace added.

"It's not even yellow," Greta complained.

"That stuff is more like pale brown," Sally put the final word on the description of the entree.

"I don't care what color it is," Aggie boasted, "I want a lot!"

"Bet you'll be sorry, Ag," Betty warned her. As Miss Fern began to dish up the plates, most of the girls asked for a little. Some asked for a medium amount. Everyone got some fruit salad and bread. When Aggie's turn came, she said,

"I want a LOT!"

Miss Fern paused with her server and stared at Aggie. "Are you sure about that, Aggie?"

"Yes! I could eat a cow!"

"That's where the gelatin came from, dear," Claire giggled. Miss Fern put a fair amount on Aggie's plate, and Aggie said she'd like a little more, a little more, while Miss Fern hesitated. Finally, she passed the plate along to Aggie.

"Try that and, if you want seconds, you may have more," Miss Fern said. Everyone dived into their supper while chatter continued about the ball game that afternoon. The little girls discussed their fun on the swings and teeter-totter. Soon, talk slowed down as everyone tackled the gelatin entree. Raw celery, green peppers, grated carrots, chopped radish, all imprisoned in unflavored gelatin turned into a rude awakening for Aggie. She forked the veggies loose from the gelatin and ate them, while she wished for some mayonnaise. She took big gulps of milk to smother the tasteless gelatin that clung to the salad.

"Please pass the pepper," she asked, and along came the pepper shaker which she used copiously to drown the generally unappetizing combination. She ate everything else, and then returned to the gelatin, now smothered in pepper.

"Miss Fern, do I have to finish all this?" Aggie pleaded.

"Yes you do. That's why you get to ask for a little or a medium amount, or a lot. But you finish what you ask for."

"I didn't know it would taste like this."

"We can't waste food. Next time, you might not be so greedy." By this stage, most of the girls had finished, but they waited, and Miss Fern waited. Aggie passed her glass for more milk, all the while wishing the glass were a cup so she could hide some of the entree. Girls began to sigh with impatience. Miss Fern looked at all the empty plates.

"Girls, as long as everyone but Aggie is finished, you may be excused to go back to your dorms." With much scraping of chairs, the girls stood and took their plates and silver to the dish wagon near the kitchen where the wash-up crew was in readiness.

Aggie sat alone at the end of the table. Miss Fern remained seated halfway down the length of the table. Aggie spread the gelatin around on her plate, in hopes that she could make it look "gone." She thought of hiding it under her plate, but it would leave a mess on the table when she took her plate to the dish wagon, and the table crew would complain to Miss Fern about the mess. Meanwhile, Miss Fern seemed to be looking everywhere, from where she sat at the table. She watched Tommy sweeping. She observed Phyllis from the first floor who was using the crumb tray and brush to make the tablecloth clean again. Denise refilled salt and pepper shakers. Aggie sat and thought hard about her dilemma. Miss Fern continued to look elsewhere.

Finally, Aggie hit upon a solution: she had two big pockets on her dress. While Miss Fern looked everywhere but at Aggie, Aggie filled her pockets with the unsavory, uneaten portion. She made scraping noises with her fork as though finally finishing. Then she drank down the rest of her milk.

"I guess I'm done, Miss Fern," Aggie announced. "May I be excused?"

"Yes, you may, Aggie. And remember, your eyes can deceive you about what you see. Next time, try a little. You may always have seconds if you like what is served." Aggie pushed her chair back and picked up her plate and silver. She was grateful that Miss Fern looked everywhere but at her because she was afraid her pockets might look lumpy or that the softening gelatin might start dampening the fabric. She marched up to the dish wagon while Miss Fern stood to leave. Miss Fern led the way out, with Aggie following. Miss Fern went ahead of her as they ascended the stairs to the second floor. Then Miss Fern turned toward her room while Aggie continued on down the hall to the bathroom. She closed the door and emptied her pockets into the toilet. The gelatin had been rubbery enough that it hadn't made any real telltale signs on the pockets, so she calmly proceeded to her room to change into pajamas for the evening. She tossed the dress down the laundry chute, and vowed never again to ask for a lot of something that looked exotic.

"Hi, pokey," Betty greeted her where she sat doing

homework. "You really almost ate a cow, at that! But I never got to eat a horse!"

"You're lucky, Bets. Just the thought of that stuff still gags me."

"Well, Ag, we warned you."

"Bet we coulda bounced it off the ceiling. Unless it stuck and dropped on somebody during the night."

"Ick. I'd rather have the cold cream. C'mon. Let's play Chinese Checkers."

Aggie's appetite returned in time for breakfast the next morning.

5 – GOT HOT ROCKS

"Ready, Aggie? We have to pick up our lunches at the dining hall, and meet the rest of the troop at the beach." Marie leaned against the door frame, cool in her sunsuit. "Sally's going to meet us at the kitchen."

"Got your swimsuit?" Aggie asked while she fished under the bed for her sandals.

"It's under my sunsuit."

Aggie threw shorts and a blouse on over her swimsuit and they dashed to the dining hall where they picked up brown paper sacks containing peanut butter sandwiches, a hard-boiled egg, an orange, and a small carton of milk. Sally was there, already peeling the egg she had retrieved from her sack.

"Hey, Sal," Marie scolded, "you won't have any lunch at our picnic if you start now!"

"Couldn't help it! Let's go before I peel the orange!" They scooted out the back door of the kitchen and giggled in anticipation of the fun ahead.

At the beach, they met their town friends and Mrs. Harper.

"A perfect day, girls! You look as though you picked up some sun at the Fourth of July celebration!"

"You're right about that, Mrs. Harper," Aggie averred. "My back is a little tender."

"Here's some lotion. You can rub some on each other's backs. Well, let's see – " Mrs. Harper consulted her watch. "There's time for a swim before our picnic, and we'll finish up our badge work on nature. Do you all have a buddy? And don't stay in too long, you'll need more lotion on those red backs!"

It was the cool part of the morning, still, and the water felt soothing on tender skin. But almost too soon, Mrs. Harper called everyone in for their picnic.

They ate lunch while Mrs. Harper pointed out the many kinds of grasses and rocks on the beach.

"Be careful not to uproot anything, but you might break off a leaf or two if you wish to study a plant. And small rocks are all right as samples," Mrs. Harper cautioned. After lunch, they wandered around among the rocks and grasses in search of more samples.

The beach party was over by mid-afternoon and everyone went off in separate directions. All except Marie and Aggie who had found the most beautiful rock of the day.

"It's such a beautiful pink!" Marie exclaimed as she ran the palm of her hand over it. "And so smooth! I never noticed how many rocks were scattered around here before, until Mrs. Harper showed us! I always rushed to get into the water."

"Yeah," Aggie added as she admired it. "And it's so big!

How will we ever get it home???!"

"HOME??" Marie sputtered. "You heard Mrs. Harper – she said SMALL rocks!"

"Well, gee, Marie, it's small compared to that one over there," Aggie pointed to a huge blue and green sedimentary rock. "And who would appreciate this rock if we left it? Nobody notices except Girl Scout troops."

"OK, Miss Smarty, how DO we get this home???"

"Roll it," Aggie responded, tucking her paper sack of samples into the waistband of her shorts. "We can add it to our rock collection."

"*Our* rock collection??"

"The one you and I started this afternoon. Oh, and the few I have on the window sill at home. Remember that flint I found on the class outing?"

"Oh, yeah. That reminds me, I have a few favorites hidden away in a drawer."

"So let's get started." Aggie picked up the rock and staggered a few feet along the beach toward the slanting road up to the streets of town.

"Here, I'll help," Marie offered. Together, they made their gasping way up the road, pausing to rest every few yards. Finally, they reached a sidewalk, and began to roll the rock toward home.

"Boy, it's getting hot!" Aggie stretched and rubbed the back of her neck.

"Do you realize, Ag, we could end up having operations all because of this rock?"

"Oh, I suppose we could. What's the name of that operation? It sounds a little like a lady's name – "

"Hernia, m'dear. I know because an uncle of mine had

one."

"We'll just roll it all the way home." So they bent over their rocky charge and rolled some more.

"My back hurts," Aggie finally complained. "Maybe we should leave it in somebody's yard. But I hate to leave something so pretty!"

"Besides, what a surprise THAT would be. And someone would complain, I'm sure." Bent over like two hairpins, they switched to rolling the rock along grassy boulevards. They took breaks to sit on the rock and pant from weariness and heat. It seemed hours before they spotted the honeysuckle bushes around the playground.

"Finally! I never want to discover another pretty rock!" Marie wheezed.

"This'll be the only one," Aggie panted. "There couldn't be another one this pretty!" They found Miss Fern and showed her their mighty discovery.

"And we didn't drop it and break it, or anything harmful!" Marie pointed out.

"But what will you do with it?" Miss Fern pondered, stroking her chin with one hand, the other hand on her hip. Just then, Greta dashed up to see what was happening. Marie told her about the rock and how hard it was to get home because it was too heavy to carry.

"Doesn't look heavy to me," Greta boasted. She lifted the rock amid a few groans and everyone tried to stop her. She then discovered she couldn't hang on to it, so she let it drop. It cracked open.

"Oh, no! Look what you've done! You've broken our rock!" Aggie shouted.

"We wanted to keep it in one piece!" Marie scolded.

"Ooooh, look," Greta marveled. "It's full of sparkles!" Everyone stopped looking at Greta and saw small fossils embedded in rock that twinkled in the sunlight.

"It's even prettier on the inside!" Marie gasped.

"And we didn't want to break it! Now we have two pieces, one for you and one for me!" Aggie added.

"I think I know what we can do, girls," Miss Fern concluded. "I know you both have other rocks in your possession. Let's start a rock exhibit in the basement. It will be your collection, but everyone can enjoy it." They carried their pieces of rock down to the basement where Miss Fern pointed out a long two-shelf bookcase, painted gray.

"There you are, you will probably want to wash these shelves before you put your rocks on them, but it's for you to use." Miss Fern turned to go upstairs, then paused. "And be sure to see me when you're all through with arranging your rocks. I have something for your sunburns."

"After this, Aggie," Marie punched her on the arm to accent her statement, "let's break open ALL the rocks we bring home."

6 – NEW DIGS

"Betty, Aggie, I've called you here to talk to you about an extra room that's opened up," Miss Fern announced as she sat at the sewing machine and pinned a hem. "Now, you two seem to get along well and have a lot of common interests. You also seem to be mature enough to be able to share a room."

Betty and Aggie looked at each other with a feeling of excitement about the possibility.

"Sure, Miss Fern," Aggie piped up.

"When can we move into our new room?" Betty asked while she bounced on her toes.

"As soon as the room is cleaned and all the storage boxes are moved out. We've found a place in the basement for those."

"Hot diggity! C'mon, Aggie, let's help clean up!" Betty

grabbed Aggie's hand and started for the door.

"Not so fast, girls!" Miss Fern stood up. "First we'll go to the broom closet and get buckets, rags, ammonia, a broom and mop. So follow me." Miss Fern led them to a closet filled with brooms, mops, brushes, rags, buckets, and cleaners. She handed each girl a bucket and rags.

"Take this ammonia, girls; and Aggie, you clean the windows. Betty, use some ammonia and clean the two cots in there. I'll get the janitor to move the boxes. Then you girls can mop. I'll find some sheets and blankets." She then led the girls down to their new room, across the hall from where they had been sleeping. Miss Fern opened the door to a room with much sunlight coming from windows on two walls. It was a corner room that promised to be filled with sunlight most of the time. A door led out to a screened porch decorated with Virginia creeper.

Excitement spurred the girls into action. Miss Fern disappeared, and they could hear her summoning the janitor on the phone. Betty and Aggie washed and dusted; and then moved their clothes into the two chests of drawers. Then they moved their crayons, paper, watercolor boxes, and stationery. Then, to help clear the room, they pushed the storage boxes into the hallway. Miss Fern appeared with sheets, blankets, and white seersucker bedspreads. She looked around and nodded her head in satisfaction at the shiny windows, clean cots, and freshly-dusted furniture.

"Well, girls, you did a good job! You may sleep in here tonight! I thought it might take another day to be ready to move in, but you've done it!" Miss Fern looked pleased.

After supper, Betty and Aggie scurried to their rooms and baptized each other in Lily of the Valley cologne to celebrate their new room. Then they exchanged trinkets to make it official.

But, after Miss Fern's goodnights, following their Bible-reading time, Betty and Aggie couldn't go to sleep. They tossed and turned and listened to crickets chirping; but they couldn't sleep.

"Aggie!" Betty whispered hoarsely.

"What?" Aggie replied.

"Guess what tune I'm tapping out." Betty's fingernails tapped out a rhythm on the metal support to her cot.

"Old McDonald?"

"No! Try again!"

"Uhhh – " Aggie listened and then guessed, "Bobby Shaftoe?"

"Yeah! Now it's your turn!"

Aggie thought a minute, then tapped out "Brahms' Lullabye."

Betty whispered one wrong answer after another, then guessed correctly just as the doorway darkened. Miss Fern's form was silhouetted against the hall light.

Aggie tried to warn Betty, whose back was to the door, but she didn't understand what Aggie was trying to say. Finally, Aggie grabbed Betty's wrist to stop her from trying to tap anything out on the bed frame.

"WHAT do you girls think you are doing? Everyone else is asleep!" Miss Fern's voice jarred them both.

"We're just trying to go to sleep," Betty responded, trying to sound sleepy.

"Would you rather go back to your old room?" Miss Fern asked.

"Oh, no! No!" Aggie and Betty exclaimed at the same

time, sitting up and rubbing their eyes.

"Then no more whispering!" Miss Fern listened at the door for a moment, and then disappeared. There was a brief silence, then Aggie said,

"I know a good story that'll put you to sleep."

"How good?"

"It's boring. You'll be asleep in no time."

"How about a ghost story?" Betty whispered. "Something creepy."

"I'd love a ghost story, but that would keep both of us awake – " Aggie heard a noise and slapped Betty's wrist to warn her. They quickly turned their backs to each other and pretended to sleep. Miss Fern's soft footsteps entered the room. She paused by Betty's bed, then turned and left. The quiet sounds of breathing soon became genuine deep sleep.

7 – ONE BIG BLISTER

Miss Fern gathered everyone together for an afternoon of picking wild strawberries. As she handed out small containers to fill, she advised the girls about poison ivy.

"You all know what poison ivy looks like, with three pointed leaves. It can grow among the strawberries, so watch where you pick. When we get home, we'll all wash with brown soap just to be sure we don't have any problems. Ready? Let's go."

Aggie quickly discovered that wild strawberries were sweeter than the store-bought kind. She ate almost as many as she put in the container. It was a beautiful afternoon in the wild, vacant lots with ripe strawberries swelling in the sun and the sound of excited voices as the "big ones" were held up for all to see. Even with all the sampling, the containers filled up, and soon Miss Fern called everyone to go home.

"We'll be back again in a few days when more berries ripen. And, with all those sidewalks to skate on, you can bring your roller skates, if you wish. Now, tonight after supper, we'll have strawberries and cream." And sure enough, after everyone washed with brown soap and ate supper, Miss Fern produced sugar and cream and, magically, little shortcakes. Enamel cups never looked so tempting as when Miss Fern filled them with strawberry shortcakes.

Full of strawberries and bedtime stories, everyone crawled into bed. Miss Fern made the rounds with cold cream and hanky rags. Once Miss Fern said her goodnights, spitballs whizzed through the air, as usual. Aggie and Betty made a contest out of who could make the most spitballs stick to the ceiling over each other's beds. Aggie soon drifted off to sleep and dreamed about strawberries until Betty shook her awake.

"Aggie, I can't sleep. I itch all over," Betty whispered.

"Didn't you wash with brown soap?" Aggie yawned.

"No. But I'll be all right. Let's go color in the bathroom."

Always ready for drawing and coloring, Aggie grabbed her paper and crayons and followed Betty to the bathroom. They each found a stall and started creating fantasies on paper.

"Pass the yellow," Betty whispered. Aggie could hear Betty scratching. She passed the yellow.

"Pass the pink," Aggie held her hand under the divider for the pink.

"Where's the red?" Betty fished through some crayons on the floor.

"Shhhh," Aggie warned. All activity ceased, including breathing. Someone was quietly approaching. Betty and Aggie strained their ears. They heard a slight scraping noise on the bathroom floor.

"Girls, what in the world are you doing?"

"Going to the bathroom," offered Aggie.

"Then whose red crayon is this? Aggie? Betty Ann?" Silence. "Both of you girls come out right now!" Miss Fern waited while Betty and Aggie gathered their crayons and paper together. They came out to face Miss Fern.

"Do you want me to move you to the Little Girls end of the dorm?"

"No," two voices chorused quietly.

"Then why don't you sleep when everyone else is sleeping?"

Aggie shrugged her shoulders. Betty began to scratch her arms.

"I couldn't sleep, Miss Fern, and I asked Aggie to keep me company. I've been itching something awful."

"Oh, no!" Miss Fern exclaimed. "Didn't you wash with brown soap?"

"No, I forgot," Betty replied.

"Betty Ann Simpson! You just might have poison ivy!" Miss Fern grabbed one of Betty's arms and took a close look at the beginnings of a rash. "Yes, you do have poison ivy! Don't scratch it! Blisters are going to form and you'll spread the rash! I'll call the clinic in the morning and get some Calamine Lotion! Now both of you go to bed! I don't know what I'm going to do with you!"

After they climbed into bed, they listened as Miss Fern's footsteps faded down the hall. Betty let out a loud sigh.

Miss Fern reminds me of Mom, Aggie pondered. *They both seem to have eyes and ears all around their heads.*

For the next few weeks, Betty's chest, arms and legs were

covered with watery blisters. She didn't feel like playing games, singing, or doing art work. She just lay around and tried not to scratch. One day, Aggie asked the question:

"Bets, why didn't you use brown soap?"

"I wanted to see what it was like to have poison ivy."

"But how did you get it under your shirt?"

"I rubbed poison ivy leaves on myself."

"Well, now you know what it's like to have poison ivy. You're one big blister."

"So do you. You've seen what it's like on me. Just don't ever rub poison ivy leaves on yourself."

8 – NEW DELIGHTS

Aggie let out a long sigh as she pulled her school dress over her head. She adjusted her new, dark blue dress with the big red tulip pocket. Then she let out another long sigh. Betty turned around and asked,

"What's THAT all about?!"

"School was awful in the city. The teachers were cranky, the schools were big and dirty, and the last one I went to was in an abandoned grocery store. I'm not ready to go back to school. But when I first started in first grade, I loved school!" Aggie arranged her tie belt and continued. "On the first school holiday, I cried 'til my eyes were bloodshot, and Mom put cold packs on my eyes. I didn't know it was a holiday and couldn't figure why school was closed that day, until Mom explained it."

"Then later, you moved to a bad school, I suppose."

"Yeah. I even skipped school at times."

Betty sat on the bed and tied her shoes.

"Well, Ag, you'll love school here. Nice teachers, clean rooms, and the townies are fun. I have lots of townie friends. Ready? C'mon, grab your skates."

"You mean we can roller skate to school?"

"Sure. C'mon, slowpoke!" Aggie caught up with Betty and they found their skates under all the coats and boots in their lockers. Everyone went out the door in a mass exodus blended with excitement. At the school grounds, the doors weren't open yet, so Betty, Aggie, Esther, and Rosie chinned themselves on the monkey bars. Soon the town kids filled the playground, and then the first bell rang.

"I'm in third grade," Aggie told a town girl who looked about her age. "Where do I go?" Betty had waved at Aggie and disappeared in a cluster of girls.

"Follow me, I'm going that way!" the girl smiled. "You're new here, aren't you? My name's Constance. What's yours?"

"Agatha. But you can call me Aggie." They hurried along toward a door at the end of the gym. Aggie breathed in the new-school-in-September smell of polish, wax, and all the other industrial-strength ingredients that tell kids they're the first ones on the scene on the first day of school.

"Our teacher's name is Miss Prescott," Constance informed Aggie. "She had second grade last year, and she moved with us. And call me Connie," she smiled in an afterthought. "Here, let's get desks together."

I'm going to like this school, Aggie thought as they pledged allegiance and sang a song she had never heard before. She looked around at all the smiling kids, the pots of bright red geraniums lining the window sills. Miss Prescott beamed at all the students who sat at freshly-varnished desks. She called roll and passed books to the students. Aggie looked around at all the new faces. A blonde girl with long, heavy braids smiled at her. Two boys named Bruce and Anthony were busy making faces at each other, and then broke down giggling in their own corner of the room. A dark-haired girl named Joanne secretly read a comic book. Morning, skating home for lunch, afternoon recess, and learning the names of kids made the day pass too quickly. At lunch, Betty had told Aggie not to wait for her because she was a fifth-grader and got out a half-hour later. Miss Fern had told Aggie not to loiter. So Aggie skipped out into the sunshine with Connie and Joanne.

"See ya tomorrow," Connie waved.

"You'll have to come over and play sometime," Joanne suggested. They headed off in different directions while Aggie tightened her roller skates and headed down the walk. To Aggie, the afternoon was magic. She took deep breaths of air filled with a pungent fragrance that had no name. Past trim lawns and quiet homes, Aggie skated until she came to a woodsy area emitting the sounds of trickling water, deep in the shadows.

A place of mystery, marveled Aggie. *Why did I miss this on the way to school or lunch? Oh – I know – I used the other side of the street!* Aggie slipped her skates off, stored them under some plants, and wended her way between birch and quaking aspen trees to a cool, quiet place where the trickling noise was louder. Aggie looked down to where a rivulet reflected the yellow and green of overhanging trees as it ran between sloping banks. She sat down on the wet, leafy mulch floor of the ravine and listened to the quiet gurgles and slurries of the rivulet. *Almost like elves and faeries talking,* she imagined.

'Course, I guess there aren't any elves and faeries. But if there were – She stood up, brushed the leaves from the back of her dress, and padded quietly between trees and small shrubs as she followed the downhill course of the rivulet until it became a faster-flowing stream that bounced over rocks. Soon, the ravine opened up and Aggie could see how it coursed toward the lake. At this point, the mossy rocks were larger, and the ground gently sloped down toward a part of the beach she had never seen before. *This really is a place of mystery. And who has decided there's no such thing as faeries and elves? Or sprites? It's the perfect place for them.* Aggie sat on a rock and drank in the scene until she realized the ravine was growing darker, and the leaves of aspen were turning from translucent sunlight to burnished gold.

She stood again, and headed back through the ravine, and scrambled up the darkened slope to where she had left her skates. She picked them up and ran home.

Miss Fern met her at the top of the stairs.

"Where have you been, young lady??" she scolded. "I looked everywhere! It's already time for dinner! Just where were you??"

"I'm sorry – I lost track of time. I was exploring. I'm really sorry!" Aggie tossed her skates into her locker.

"You have scratches all over your arms and legs! Where

were you exploring, to get all scratched up like that? And just look at your new school dress!" So Aggie explained about the mystery place she had found, how beautiful it all was, and how easy it was to lose track of time. Miss Fern listened closely, then ordered, "Wash up! And after this, get home when you're supposed to!" Miss Fern's blue eyes snapped behind her glasses.

Boyoboy! I've never seen Miss Fern this mad! Aggie felt hot all over from the scolding. She hurried to wash up and change clothes before joining everyone for dinner.

"So! Did you find anything really, truly interesting?" Betty teased. "I mean, besides making Miss Fern awfully mad!"

"I didn't find any poison ivy," Aggie retorted.

"Well, Ag, you made an interesting first day at school!"

Next day, Aggie met more townies and realized she was really going to love going to school. How could you not love going to a school surrounded by green lawn and hedges, petunias in flower beds, bright geraniums on the window sills, and a playground filled with wondrous ways to risk one's life?

But when the last bell rang, Aggie hurriedly said goodbye to new friends, and RAN home. She arrived out of breath, wheezing as she climbed the stairs to the second floor.

Miss Fern could hear the wheezing, and met Aggie at the top of the stairs.

"My goodness, Aggie, your face is all red! Did you run all the way? I didn't mean for you to do that!" Miss Fern's eyes showed alarm, and Aggie thought she might have seen a bit of sympathy. "I only meant, Aggie, that you not dawdle the rest of the afternoon away! You can walk or even skate home! Just get home at a reasonable time! I don't want to have to worry about you!" Miss Fern felt Aggie's forehead. "You ARE hot! Go throw some cold water on your face, change clothes, and come downtown with me! We'll get a library card for you! Miss Fensmore is taking care of the younger girls."

Aggie hurried through washing her face and changing clothes, then joined Miss Fern on a leisurely walk down to the library. While she checked out some books on her new library card, Miss Fern went to the store and met Aggie outside.

"Here, Aggie, I got this for you, and I got one for myself," Miss Fern smiled. She handed a mint patty to Aggie. Aggie held it in her hand and stared at its silver wrapper with the blue lettering. It was a big mint patty, and Aggie unwrapped it slowly, savoring a delicious moment, almost hesitant to take the first bite. Miss Fern had already bitten into her own mint confection, so Aggie finally decided to hurry and catch up.

9 – "THE LONE RANGER," IN A NUTSHELL

The signs were all around – leaves fell in bright red, lemon yellow, golden yellow, orange, and burnished mahogany; the Virginia creeper turned fiery red; there was an afternoon of picking and storing apples in the basement; and the shagbark hickory trees dropped nuts onto the ground. The afternoon shadows looked different to Aggie, and the days seemed shorter. It was autumn.

Miss Fern approached the older girls about fudge. If they could pick and shell the hickory nuts, she would make fudge on her hotplate, and they could listen to "The Lone Ranger."

Miss Fern's offer turned into enormous fun. After all, there were all those bright leaves to rustle through in search of nuts while the afternoon sun filtered through the leaves that still clung to the branches and released a pungent aroma not smelled at any other time of the year. At times, Aggie discovered nuts because she knelt on them. Other times, she felt lucky just to find them under that colorful blanket of oak and maple leaves. She also pocketed acorns, hoping Miss Fern could tell her how to make buttons out of the caps. Aggie filled the old lard bucket that Miss Fern had given her for collecting the nuts. Aggie pulled her sweater under her so she could sit in the leaves and feel how alive the earth beneath her really was; how the energy given off was part of herself. She inhaled the smells from the warm afternoon. Not far away, Betty and Sally rolled in the leaves, threw fistfuls at each other, and splashed them heavenward as though they played in water. The sun caught the colors as the leaves swirled up and then floated down again, only to be tossed upward into the sunlight again. In another direction, Pat and Shirley tried to make angels in the leaves as they lay on their backs and moved their arms up and down, giggling in enjoyment.

"C'mon, daydreamer," Claire called as she approached Aggie.

"Looks like you found a lot!" Aggie jumped to her feet.

"Yeah, so did you!" Aggie grabbed Claire's hand to steady herself and brush the bits of leaves off her clothes. Then she stooped to pick up her can of nuts. By then, Betty and Sally joined them as they hurried back to the dorm. Pat and Shirley hurried to catch up.

That evening, Miss Fern spread newspapers on the floor of her room. She handed out a couple of hammers, some pliers, and a few rocks to pound the shells open and pry the nut meats out. She placed an earthenware bowl among them. Everyone fell to work on the nuts, saving the picking of nut meats for when it was time to hear the Lone Ranger and Tonto in a breathtaking adventure. Soon, the pounding was over, and all was silent as Miss Fern tuned the radio to the right station. The theme song for "The Lone Ranger" floated out of the decorative cloth behind the carved wood of the desktop radio. The girls quietly picked the nut meats out of their hiding places and tossed them into the bowl. They listened so intently to the radio drama that they hardly noticed Miss Fern stirring ingredients in a pan on the hotplate until the exquisite smell of cooking chocolate passed under their noses.

"Someone, pass that bowl to me," Miss Fern whispered while she kept on stirring. She had turned off the heat and was testing the cooling mixture.

"Tune in tomorrow for another adventure of 'The Lone Ranger and Tonto,'" the radio's message intoned. The girls sighed. Miss Fern finally decided it was time to add the nuts and stir everything together.

"If you girls get your homework done in time tomorrow night, I'll let you hear another story about the Lone Ranger," Miss Fern promised while she smoothed the fudge into a greased pie plate. Excited whispers followed. The girls carefully rolled the newspapers together, catching all the nutshells inside.

"Just put it all in the wastebasket over there," Miss Fern indicated with a nodding head while she continued to smooth the fudge. "And wash your hands before tasting this fudge," she added. They took turns using Miss Fern's sink. Then came the magic time, cutting and tasting the fudge with much licking of fingers. Miss Fern covered the fudge after everyone had a second piece.

"We must save some for the younger girls," Miss Fern explained.

"Yum! When can we do this again?" Sally asked. All the voices chimed in,

"Yes! When??"

"Oh, we'll probably do this again soon. But tomorrow night, after your homework is done, we'll hear 'The Lone Ranger' again." It was official: "The Lone Ranger" would be the evening bedtime story for the older girls who could stay up longer than the younger girls who would still get their bedtime story, as well.

A few weeks later, it was fudge night again. Very quietly, the girls cracked nuts and picked out the nut meats. The Lone Ranger and Tonto continued to bring mesmerizing drama into Miss Fern's room. The chocolatey treat that followed made for sweet dreams.

But one night, after the last of the nuts had been used in one final batch of creamy fudge, after enough had been set aside to share with the younger girls, after the radio had advised its listeners to "tune in tomorrow night," Miss Fern tucked the girls in, and distributed the usual dobs of cold cream and hanky rags. Bets and Ag tossed their spitballs up to the ceiling, and they could hear all the giggles across the hall as their pals did the same thing.

All was quiet. Until the phone in the hall jarred everyone awake. They could hear Miss Fern's footsteps approaching the shrill instrument on the wall.

"Ag, who could be calling so late at night?" Bets hissed.

"It's not really late – just late to us," Aggie yawned. "Shhhh, listen!" They heard Miss Fern replying to the voice on the line.

"I don't see what harm a little fun like fudge and 'The Lone Ranger' are going to do to these girls!" Miss Fern exclaimed. There was silence from Miss Fern as she listened on receiver. "Oh, yes, Miss Conrad, I know you're the nurse and concerned about their sleep, their health, and all that; but I'm their mother! And their happiness must be considered, too! This might be an institution, but we shouldn't institutionalize any of the children living here! It's better to lose a little sleep for some innocent entertainment than to march in lockstep! And that's it – in a nutshell! Good night!" Betty and Aggie heard the receiver jammed into its cradle. They listened as Miss Fern's footsteps retreated to her room.

"Bets! Did you hear all that? Did you?" Aggie was up and shaking Betty by the shoulders.

"Of *course*, I heard it all!" Betty grabbed Aggie by the arms and they found themselves hugging and giggling. Suddenly, Shirley, Claire, Pat and Sally bounced onto Betty's bed.

"Did you hear *that??*" Sally exclaimed.

"She stood up to the sternest person on the grounds!" Pat exclaimed in a hoarse whisper.

"Yeah! I've never seen Miss Conrad smile!" Shirley added.

"Not even when she gives us cod liver oil!" Claire laughed. "I was just remembering when she gave us green soap instead of cod liver oil!"

"And she called us all back 'n' asked if we felt all right!" Betty recalled.

"They sure don't taste the same! But the color is almost identical – except green soap is just a little greener!" Aggie rolled with a choked giggle.

"Really, it's funny we didn't get sick!" Betty concluded. "I wonder if she ever has any fun!"

"I'd be surprised," Claire sounded almost sympathetic. "C'mon, kiddos, we better get back to bed before Miss Fern hears us. We might lose 'Lone Ranger' privileges!"

"G'night," Betty hissed. "And that's it, in a nutshell!" Just as Aggie turned over with a sigh, a gooey glob dropped on her face. A spitball.

10 – SEW A FINE SEAM

A new girl moved into the room where Betty and Aggie used to sleep. Her name was Yvonne. She was a dark-haired pixie with a cheerful attitude and infectious sense of humor. Her grandmother was an older version of Yvonne. On Sundays, when most of the girls had visitors who brought cookies or candy, Yvonne's grandmother usually brought jars of pickles, baked ham, canned pigs' knuckles, and other delicacies. But one Sunday, she brought several yards of heavy pink satin – the kind of satin that, to Aggie, looked good enough to eat. It wasn't "nursery pink" – it wasn't "strawberry pink" – it was more the kind of luscious pink that royalty would wear. The yardage had body. It weighed more than the kind of satin of which slips and nightgowns are made. Aggie just had to hold it in her hands.

Aggie knew that satin of that quality had to be made into SOMETHING. Aggie asked Yvonne if she would like a ball gown. Of course, Yvonne would like a ball gown!

"Supreme!" She laughed and jumped up and down at the prospect. One day, Yvonne dragged the yardage out of its hiding place. For a little while, Aggie held the shimmering yardage in her lap and ran her hands over its smooth weight, while she gazed at its luscious pinkness; then she found pins in the sewing room, and the two girls set themselves to the creative task of styling a ball gown. They sketched and resketched and finally hit upon a simple and elegant dream of a dress.

"Fancy!" Yvonne giggled the word in her excitement. She stood still as a statue while Aggie pinned the fabric in pleats and darts to fit Yvonne. Finally, the task was done, and Yvonne looked ready for a fairy-tale waltz in a dream castle. Yvonne giggled and twirled.

"I love it," Yvonne rhapsodized. "Just love it!" But Aggie realized there was a problem: how to get the dress off Yvonne and ready for sewing. Miss Fern came upon this pink satin scene and stopped, stock still.

"It's beautiful, girls! But there is a problem. I'm going to have to give you sewing lessons!" Miss Fern turned Yvonne one way and another. "Come with me," Miss Fern continued. Down the hall to the sewing room the three proceeded. She fished through the cupboards until she found some patterns.

"Now, girls, these are slip patterns. I'll find some material – " Miss Fern searched through another cupboard and brought out some used sheets. "The first thing you will learn is how to cut out a pattern to fit you, and to cut it in such a way that it won't sag or twist."

Day followed day as Miss Fern taught Yvonne and Aggie how to cut "on the straight of the fabric," how to make French seams, and how to use bias tape around the arm holes and neck opening. She then gave each girl an embroidery pattern for decorations on each slip. Meanwhile, Miss Fern finished the pink satin "gown" the girls had dreamed up. Yvonne laid it lovingly in a drawer.

One Sunday, Yvonne took the dress to show her grandmother. Then Yvonne hurriedly brought ham, pickles, cheese and a loaf of dark bread to Miss Fern to keep for her before she ran back to finish visiting with her grandmother. Miss Fern promised that she would put the ham in the cooler in the dining hall, 'til they were ready to share it. That was the last time the girls ever saw Yvonne. She ran away with her grandmother and no one could trace her. At least not right away – and if anyone ever talked to her grandmother, none of the girls in Miss Fern's group ever heard about it. Still, Aggie remembered a scrumptious, edible-pink ball gown, fit for a princess.

11 – SWEET VALENTINES

Hearts and flowers. Lacy-edged messages. Heart-shaped lollipops. Everyone at home and at school worked hard on valentines. In Aggie's fourth-grade class, Miss Truett set out a big, fancy box with hearts all over it, and a slit on top, so boys and girls could drop their valentines into the box for Miss Truett to distribute on Valentine's Day. Each day, more valentines dropped through the slot.

At home, an occasional love song poured out of Miss Fern's radio. Miss Fern seemed busy cutting and pasting, but no one really barged into her room to see what she was doing. But everyone found out on Valentine's Day when she presented each girl with a bright valentine made of red gumdrops glued to a card in the form of a heart surrounded by paper lace. Miss Fern's labors were greeted with awe and appreciation. Also temptation to eat the gumdrops; but Miss Fern reminded the girls that the candy was glued to the cards with that awful, smelly, yellow glue that wasn't good for anyone. The gumdrops were strictly ornamental. Still, twelve girls treasured what Miss Fern had done. Soon, each locker door boasted a sweet, bright-red gumdrop valentine. Rosie stood back and admired the effect then said,

"I'm so glad I got in on one more Valentine's Day before leaving to live with my aunt!" Rosie had packed most of her things and was ready to leave on Friday.

Valentine's Day at school was just as exciting. Everyone in Aggie's class opened valentines from everyone else. Some valentines were quite special because they were fancy, lace-edged, and sentimental. Aggie opened two of those special valentines and read boys' names after the surprisingly love-y messages. She realized that the same boys who threw crab apples and balls of sticky burdock at her on the way home were the same boys who sent lacy valentines. Miss Truett passed a tray of heart cookies. Fourth-grade-love was in the air.

By Friday, Aggie raced home to play marbles with Bets who was playing for keeps with everyone who challenged her. Aggie had been practicing and hoped to regain some of her earlier losses. But something was different when she got to her locker. She saw a blank valentine. All the other valentines looked just as blank. All the valentines that Miss Fern had made were now denuded of red gumdrop hearts. Only a few spots of glue remained.

"Who did this??!" Aggie asked around. One of the little girls piped up,

"Rosie did it just before she left. I watched her."

Aggie stared at the valentine wreckage. Then she asked the little girl,

"Did Rosie see you watching her?"

"Oh, she didn't care if I watched. I was sorta hiding, but she saw me, and didn't care."

"Well, she was leaving anyway. What could we do about it?"

"She did leave some of the glue," came the reply.

"But not all of it," Aggie observed. *Yechhhh! Glue and gumdrops! What a flavor combination!*

12 – THE ALL-NIGHT EASTER BUNNY

"Good news, girls," Miss Fern sang out as she entered the parlor where Betty made paper dolls, Alice perused a movie magazine, Sally and Greta listened to the radio, Aggie drew fantasy fashions and Rosie worked on a school assignment. All activity ceased as Miss Fern set the box on a table. "You all get new Easter clothes!"

Group gasp. It was hard for anyone to talk, so squeals of excitement did the job as Miss Fern opened the box and began to pull beautiful dresses out of layers of tissue paper. Ooooh's and aaaah's followed each revelation of taffeta, moire, voile, and organdy. Girls held dresses up to themselves and swapped with each other.

"I might have to pin some hems or make some alterations, but I don't think there are many changes to make," Miss Fern smiled at the sight of so many delighted girls twirling and posing like models. There was really hardly anything to do except for a few hems, as each girl found the perfect fit and style, and hung her amazing Easter fashion in the closet. How could anyone wait for Easter? It was only three days away. All the girls would go to the Easter service in new finery!

But on Friday, Miss Fern called everyone together with sad news: the dresses had to go back! They had been sent to the wrong place! No one could talk. Disappointment hung on the air like invisible tears. Then, everyone swallowed the pain and became young philosophers about the fashion tragedy. After all, there were other nice things in those closets. One by one, the dresses came back to Miss Fern who looked as sad as all the girls. She counted the dresses to be sure she had the right number, slowly closed the flaps of the box, and took it to the administration building, while everyone watched her from the parlor windows.

Night came. The hall was the most quiet that Aggie had ever remembered. Miss Fern made her loving rounds, doled out dobs of cold cream and hanky rags; but it was hard to get up the enthusiasm for making spitballs. Soon, everyone was asleep; but Aggie kept dreaming to a humming sound. Was it an airplane flying through her dream? Sometimes it stopped, and then started again. Aggie woke up intermittently, realizing that Miss Fern was in the sewing room on the other side of the wall. Then she drifted off to sleep again. Finally, she woke up with the knowledge that it was really late at night, but Miss Fern was still sewing. She was sewing very fast. Was this going to go on all night? Would Miss Fern ever stop, and go to bed? How could anyone stay up all night? Even Betty and Aggie couldn't stay awake all night! Aggie noticed that all that sewing didn't disturb Bets.

Next morning, Aggie found out why Miss Fern hadn't slept. She presented each of the girls with an Easter dress. Where had she gotten them? How did she know everyone's sizes so well? She never said. She just said that the "Easter Bunny" did it.

Of course, everyone knew the Easter Bunny was Miss Fern. They knew by Miss Fern's dimpled smile and the twinkle in her eyes.

And Aggie knew because of a night filled with the sounds of a humming sewing machine.

13 – IT'S ALL IN YOUR HEAD

"Miss Conrad, I don't feel so good," Aggie stood before Miss Conrad, the nurse. "Miss Fern sent me down to see what's wrong."

"You look all right to me," Miss Conrad replied. She took a close look at Aggie, studied her arms and face, and then looked into her throat. "I think it's all in your head."

"I'm sure it's not in my head," Aggie insisted. She sniffled so her nose wouldn't drip. "I just don't feel good."

"Just go back to your dorm. I think you might just have a light bout of sniffles. Concentrate on something else." Miss Conrad's mouth formed a straight line, as she gave two soda pills to Aggie.

"OK, Miss Conrad," Aggie shrugged her shoulders and

left.

Next day at school, Aggie still didn't feel good, but she carried a hanky for her sniffles. Her throat began to ache.

"Where's Joanne?" she asked Nancy at recess.

"She has the measles. She's out of school for a week or two," came the reply.

By lunchtime, Aggie noticed some spots on her arms. Miss Fern looked at Aggie and said,

"Go down to the clinic. I'm afraid you might be coming down with the measles."

At the clinic, Miss Conrad peered into Aggie's throat, noted her runny nose, and said,

"Looks like measles. I suppose you've exposed most of the school!"

"No, Miss Conrad, other kids from town have measles already."

"Follow me. I'll assign a bed for you. We'll get a toothbrush for you later." Aggie followed Miss Conrad to a four-bed ward and took a bed near the window. Miss Conrad pulled the shades.

"You can't have a lot of light," she told Aggie crisply. Still no smile.

Gee, I miss the kids and Miss Fern already. So quiet in here! I wonder if any more kids will get measles. Aggie wiggled her toes under the cool sheets and thought about her friends at school. Miss Conrad came in with a toothbrush, toothpaste, and water. She popped a thermometer under Aggie's tongue and left. It seemed a long time before Miss Conrad returned, this time with another girl, Barbara, from the first floor in the girls' dorm.

"Another measles case to keep you company," Miss

Conrad announced.

"Hi, Barb," Aggie greeted her. Then she fell asleep. It was late afternoon when Miss Conrad woke her with a dinner tray. When morning came, Louise from Barb's floor joined the group. After lunch, Greta took the fourth bed. Across the hall, boys were taking up bed space. During the days, when Aggie felt like sleeping most of the time, she could tell when Miss Conrad was coming down the hall or entering their ward because of her starched white uniform. Her nurse's cap sat securely fastened on her head by bobby pins that matched her wavy brown hair. She looked at all the kids through her silver-rimmed glasses, and her thin face rarely expressed an emotion.

"Next, I'll have to start filling the sunroom," Miss Conrad sighed. Sure enough, in a few days the sunroom was almost filled with coughing, sniffly kids. Miss Conrad brought games and puzzles to the other two wards.

"Won't someone catch measles when we handle these?" Louise asked. Miss Conrad shook her head.

"No – once you're over the sniffles and sneezing, and after you break out in spots, you won't spread it."

Into the second week, everyone was trading games and puzzles, joking and laughing. Aggie could hardly wait to get out and see Miss Fern and all her friends again. One day, Miss Conrad came into the ward to look at everyone's spots.

"I'm about over the measles," Aggie exclaimed.

"Almost, but not quite," Miss Conrad sighed while she turned Aggie's arms over and squinted at the fading spots. "Maybe in a day or two, you can go home." That was a blow to Aggie who felt ready for the playground and school again.

"I'm bored," she pouted after Miss Conrad left. "I'm over

the measles and ready to leave!" Then she thought, *If Miss Conrad thinks this was all in my head, maybe getting rid of the measles for good is also in my head!* She sat and concentrated on the spots being gone. She even squeezed her eyes shut to picture clear arms and face. She almost got grumpy, she tried so hard at thinking herself rid of all the spots.

When Miss Conrad brought lunch, she stopped and looked at Aggie again. Miss Conrad had a blank look on her face. Then she announced,

"After lunch, Aggie, you may go home." Aggie wasn't sure if all that concentration made the difference, or if the spots would have gone away in due time that day. All she knew was that she had given it her best shot.

Home again! I missed seeing everyone, and school, and the playground! And Miss Fern. And throwing spitballs!

Aggie packed up and said goodbye, then headed for the door. She was sure she saw dimples on the corners of Miss Conrad's mouth. And she was certain that it wasn't all in her head.

14 – THE CHOCOLATE BURIAL

The egg, made of hollow chocolate and decorated with pink and white flowers and green leaves, rested in a nest of green grass inside a box decorated with eggs and bunnies. It was the most beautiful Easter surprise Aggie had ever received. Needless to say, Aggie was ready to dive into the first bite, yet hesitant to mar the beauty of such a delectable confection. To eat that delicacy alone was unthinkable in a life of Group-Everything, done in hordes, bunches, cliques, and clusters: group meals, assembled prayer, harmonized singing, and mob recreation. One shared such a treat, because it was an occasion that rarely happened – the occasion of EATING SWEETS. The girls often heard how sweets could rot one's teeth or ruin complexions. Cavities and zits. So, with the arrival of this lovely Easter egg, twelve excited girls gathered around Miss Fern while she carefully cut dainty bites to pass around. Then she carefully closed the decorative box over the remainder of the egg, and placed it on a shelf in her sewing room.

"There will be more another time," she explained, as she nibbled a refined bit of chocolate. "You don't want to ruin your supper – OR your complexions."

So, every few days, Miss Fern took the box from its shelf, and all twelve girls group-died over the ecstasy of letting bits of chocolate melt on their tongues and roll about in their mouths. They knew how to get the most from the moment. Then came the Saturday morning when Miss Fern called the girls together to cut up the last of the egg – the thickest part. The girls swarmed together for those final bites of velvety provender. They jiggled and giggled in expectant glee while Miss Fern slowly drew the box from her sewing cupboard. All talk and teasing stopped. A dozen pairs of eyes fastened on her hands as she carefully lifted the lid. Then she stepped back, her hands paused in mid-air, and her face took on a horrified expression. All eyes riveted on a recumbent mouse lying in furry peace, its peach-toned belly protruding, its ears forever deaf to the gasps of disappointment and revulsion, followed by stunned silence. All stared at the stiff tail and curled toes of the small creature.

Then a voice rescued the moment: "He died happy."
Said another, "We should have a funeral."
"Yeah. Have a funeral. But the dead hasta have a name."
"Uh – Sparky."
"Naw – how about Fuzzball?"
"Squeaky."
"Ya. Squeaky."
"Sure. Why not?"
"We need a funeral director, too."

"Someone dignified. Who could that be?"

After all the discussion, the choice came down to Esther, without doubt the most dignified, to conduct the last rites.

"Girls, you must do this fast!" Miss Fern ordered.

That very afternoon, everyone gathered around the deceased who lay in his chocolate coffin, surrounded by the shredded green grass, inside the decorative box. Esther's freckles stood out on her naturally pale face; her red-gold hair was combed more carefully than usual. She delivered a proper eulogy about Squeaky, who knew a good thing when he saw it. She enlarged on how he lived life to the fullest and that's why he over-ate and thus died a happy death.

After one more hymn, all the girls bowed their heads while Esther intoned a prayer for Squeaky who had gone to a chocolate end because he didn't know how to stretch a tidbit by letting it melt in his mouth and roll around on his tongue. And he had no worries about cavities and zits. Then it was time to march out to the playground in solemn procession to the honeysuckle hedge.

Esther gravely led the interment proceedings as each girl sprinkled dirt over Squeaky's resting place. They tamped the dirt with their sturdy, sensible, lace-up shoes and said goodbye to Squeaky and the chocolate egg forever – or so everyone thought.

Not long after, Aggie skipped home through a pale green afternoon with happy thoughts of peril on the trapeze or the violence of a softball game. But the preschoolers were inhabiting the playground. A knot of little kids clustered suspiciously near Squeaky's grave. Aggie raced over. A hole in the ground gaped mockingly. Aggie stared at the small faces which beamed at her through chocolate-coated smiles.

"We heard about the candy," one of them commented.

"What did you do with the mouse?" Aggie asked in disbelief.

"Oh – we played with the mouse for awhile. Somebody musta throwed it away." His words melted in the candy he savored by licking all around his mouth.

"That canny was aw-wful good. Yoo shoonta buried it," a small girl admonished through glossy, chocolate lips.

"You dumb kids can get sick doing stuff like this!" Aggie scolded.

"No, we can't," an older, wiser five-year-old opined. "We jus' had our vak-sin-nations!"

15 – A PLAYMATE'S DEPARTURE

It was June, school was out, and tonsillectomy season had begun. The younger children had rides to the city, stayed for a few days, and then returned with sore throats and talked about the ice cream. Aggie was glad she had had her tonsils out before she came to live with Miss Fern. She remembered how sore her throat had been, how the other kids had throats more sore than hers, and how she ate any ice cream the other kids had given her because they couldn't swallow.

Tonsillectomies were the harbinger of summer, along with more softball games, strawberry picking, lots of roller skating, swimming, summertime birthdays, and Fourth of July. Aggie had already been to birthday celebrations at the homes of some of the townies. Those were great fun, lasted all afternoon, and Aggie always returned too full to eat supper. Aggie learned to ride a bike at Joanne's birthday party, and from then on, she prayed for a bicycle of her own.

Yet, the birthday celebrations that really stood out in

Aggie's mind were the ones that Miss Fern celebrated with the girls. There was always a special cake. Aggie wrapped a birthday gift for Ann while she thought about her own birthday celebration with a coconut cake during the previous autumn. Alice had been so excited about the party, she almost dropped the cake plate on the floor, but everyone saw what was happening and rescued the cake, as well as the occasion. Then came Claire's party with chocolate cake. Miss Fern always stuck little surprises in the cakes and told the girls what they stood for: a thimble meant the girl would be a spinster; a ring meant she'd get married; a penny predicted riches. All the girls enjoyed the fun. The birthday girl received little gifts her friends had found among their treasures hidden away in the dresser drawers.

"Bets, what are you giving to Ann?" Aggie asked as she put the finishing touch to the blue bow that held the bright paper decorated with clowns and balloons.

"I'm giving her some of my marbles. What are you giving her?"

"Some barrettes I've hardly used. They don't stay in my hair." Aggie thought about Ann, how shy she was, yet she always smiled at everyone. Aggie had enjoyed pushing her in the swings on the playground, or showing her how to hang from the ringers. Ann had also just learned to roller skate. There was something about the charm of Ann that made the older girls want to pick her up and carry her around. She almost reached the point where there were too many hugs, too much carrying.

Miss Fern's voice carried all the way down the hall to announce that it was time for the party. Footsteps from all the rooms converged on the parlor where the big, round table was decorated with a paper cloth and paper plates. In the middle stood a lemon cake frosted with vanilla icing. Miss Fern planted seven candles on the cake. She struck a match, lit the candles, and everyone made the hall ring with a lusty rendition of "Happy Birthday." After Ann stood up and blew the candles out, Miss Fern cut the cake and everyone looked for the surprises she had inserted beforehand.

"Oh, you're going to be a lawyer," Miss Fern announced to Greta. "And, Alice, you'll be a schoolteacher."

"Oh, Bets," Aggie gasped. "You're going to be rich!"

"Has anyone found the ring?" Miss Fern inquired. "Oh! It's Ann! She's going to get married!"

"Looks like I'm going to be an old maid," Shirley laughed as she held up the thimble, for all to see.

"I can imagine!" Greta exclaimed. "With your naturally curly hair, and little feet and perfect face!"

"Well, you're pretty too," Shirley insisted. "Hey, Ann! Are you going to open your presents?" The girls grew quiet and expectant as Ann began to peel the paper away from the first surprise. Oooh's and aaah's followed.

"I'll show you how to play marbles and WIN!" Betty told Ann when she opened the little bag that Betty had given her. Ann smiled and said a soft "thank you" with each revelation uncovered inside the bright paper.

Cries of "Open mine next!" went up whenever Ann reached for another package. The last package was wrapped in pink tissue paper. It was sweet-smelling soap from Miss Fern. Of course, everyone ate more cake.

"Whose birthday is next?" Miss Fern asked.

"Beverly's!" a voice replied.

"Beverly's birthday is a month away, yet. And our new

girl, Marcia, had her sixth birthday right before she came to us from Jefferson Hall," Miss Fern noted. "Isn't that right, Marcia?" Marcia nodded while she forked another bit of cake into her mouth. "Well, it won't be long before we have another one, I'm sure!"

A few weeks later, Miss Fern gathered her charges together to say goodbye to the girls who were to have their tonsils out. The boys from Harper Hall had just returned and were still too sore to talk. Everyone hugged Beverly, Greta, Ann, and Pat.

"Hurry back," Miss Fern urged each girl as she hugged them. "We'll miss each one of you."

"Eat lots of ice cream," Aggie hollered as they all departed.

"I'm surprised you're so skinny," Bets observed. "You have such a big appetite."

"Think how skinny I'd be if I didn't have an appetite," Aggie retorted. "Let's get up a softball game. The boys are going to play too, cuz their playground is being tarred and graveled. Let's see if we can beat 'em!"

A few days later, Beverly, Greta, and Pat returned. Miss Fern called the girls together in the parlor. She sat down on the sofa and asked the girls to gather closer.

"Girls, I have some sad news. Ann died. It happened while she was still under anesthesia. I'm so sorry to have to tell you this. I know you have all lost family members in the past. And usually those were older relatives, like a grandparent or someone else who was older than you. But I don't think you have lost many playmates close to your age." Miss Fern kept her composure but looked pale and sad. She squeezed a white hanky in one fist. Stunned silence followed her announcement. A voice piped up.

"Is she in Heaven now?"

"Yes, dear."

"Gosh, I was going to teach her to win at marbles!" Betty whispered.

"It seems so strange. I used to push her in the swing, and now she's gone!" Aggie whispered back.

"She got a ring in her birthday cake. She was going to get married," Marcia's high voice broke the silence.

"Maybe people can get married in Heaven," Sally offered consolation.

"Well, girls, that's all I can say right now. Let's remember how much we enjoyed knowing Ann while we could." Miss Fern stood to let the girls know there wasn't any more to add. "If any of you find you are troubled and want to talk, just come to me."

Back in their rooms, Betty and Aggie sat on their beds and stared into space. Sally appeared in the doorway.

"C'n I come in?"

"Sure," the two girls replied in unison. Sally plopped down on the edge of Betty's bed and faced Aggie.

"We need to practice for the Fourth of July races, Ag," Sally announced. "You and I always win the playground races, and we can win money in the races at the town park."

"You usually win, Sal."

"But we're so close at the end of the race. One of us should win! Unless there's a townie who's faster, but I don't know of any!"

Aggie thought it over. *Sally is so wiry*, she pondered. *No fat on her at all. Maybe she cuts the breeze better, like some sort of greyhound. But I'm skinny too. Maybe there's a chance.*

Miss Fern's voice cut through the silence. "It's time to go to the dining hall for lunch."

"Maybe this afternoon, Sal." Aggie decided. "We'll race each other then."

Strange how life just keeps on, even when friends disappear out of it. There's always something to keep one's mind on the next moment. Any of us can disappear out of all the activity at any time. Aggie ran to the bathroom to cry into a washcloth. A few of the other girls were already there, splashing water on their reddened eyes and tear-streaked faces.

16 – TWILIGHT'S LAST GLEAMING

"Wake up, Aggie! Isn't this the day you wear your pleated wallpaper?" Betty shook her. She also giggled. Aggie stretched.

"What? Pleated what?"

"It's the Fourth of July! Did you forget?"

"Fourth of July! I gotta hurry!" Aggie jumped out of bed and began dressing. "And we're all wearing our roller skates with our pleated wallpaper, in the parade! I wish you were in it with me, Bets!"

"I'll see you at the park after the parade! How many of you Girl Scouts are going to be there?" Betty was in her shorts and blouse and was tying her shoes.

"Let's see – along with Mrs. Harper – well, she's just going to watch us today – there's Marie and Sally, and the rest are the townies – Joanne, Prudence, Elizabeth, – and – uh, Eleanor, and Janice."

"Do I get to see your skirt?"

"Mrs. Harper has all of them. We made them at our last meeting." Aggie replied breathlessly. "She's keeping them 'til just before the parade."

"It's time for breakfast, so let's go!"

"I'm almost too excited to eat!"

"But Miss Fern said we all have to have a good breakfast!"

"I know, I know – "

Aggie had no idea so many people would be in the parade.

"Looks like everybody in town is marching. Who's going to watch us?" she asked Janice.

"You'd be surprised! People from other towns come here! Hey, Ag, your skirt is crooked. Here, I'll help you – "

"Ready with the skates?" Mrs. Harper came by and gave approving nods. "All right, girls, Marie and Joanne will carry our Scout banner, and everyone get in line behind them. Don't straggle. I'll see you at the park."

The school band led off with drums and piccolos, sending a trill of marching cadence through the air. Then came the Legionnaires, then the town fire engine. After that came an out-of-town band with trumpets and trombones, then the Kiwanis Club, the local equestrian club, some other school groups, the Girl Scouts, Brownies, then some town dignitaries, the Boy Scouts, Cub Scouts, and the Mayor riding in a convertible.

Lots of people on the curbs! thought Aggie. *Janice was right! What a day it will be at the park! And our skirts look pretty good!*

At the park, Mrs. Harper snapped pictures with her

Brownie camera.

"I'll get these printed as soon as possible, girls, and remember – day after tomorrow is our beach picnic!"

Aggie hurried to remove her skirt and get ready for the race with Sally. It would be one of the first races. Then there would be the three-legged race with Shirley for a partner, and there would be hot dogs, ice cream, bingo, dunk the clown, a bean bag throw for prizes, darts for prizes, a softball game with the Kiwanis men against the Legionnaires, and movies that night, along with fireworks.

But, for Aggie, the challenge of the day was the race with Sally. Others would be in the race, but she had raced the others before – and won. Only Sally remained for her to beat. Soon the announcer called for race entrants, and the runners lined up. Aggie stood next to Sally.

"On your mark, get set, GO!" And the runners thundered off along the track. Aggie gave it her all. She took a quick glance at Sally right beside her, with legs like pistons, chest out, chin in the air, black silky hair straight back in the breeze.

How does she do it? She's all sinew, she runs like a whippet.

Briefly, Aggie pulled ahead, but then Sally poured on the steam and gained on her. Friends on the sidelines were screaming,

"C'mon, Sal!"

"C'mon, Ag!"

"Go get 'em, Connie!"

Other names were being shouted as well, while Aggie tried to hold her own beside Sally. It seemed as though Sally won "by a nose."

"Good going, Ag," Sally smiled between gulps of air.

"You won again, Sal!" Aggie grinned.

"Good try, kiddo, and I liked those pleated skirts!" It was Betty, appearing out of the crowd. "Let's go get a hot dog."

Later, Shirley and Aggie felt lucky just to keep from falling in the three-legged race. Betty entered with a townie friend named Linda and came in second.

By the end of the day, the movies were punctuated by little dots of light in the air. Miss Fern came and sat down on the cool grass to watch the movies with Betty, Clair, Shirley, Marie, and Aggie.

"Those are lightning bugs, sometimes known as fireflies," she explained when Aggie seemed puzzled by the little blinking punctuations of light in the night air.

"As pretty as fireworks," Marie commented.

"I'd like to catch some in a jar," Aggie exclaimed.

"What then?" Miss Fern asked. "They'd die."

"Oh, I wouldn't want that to happen It just seemed like a nice souvenir of a wonderful day."

All the way home, after the fireworks, Aggie enjoyed the familiar sound of the chirping crickets in the sweet night air; and the gleaming dots of lightning bugs made sparks in the air as the last hint of light in the west disappeared.

Only one thing left to cap off this perfect day, thought Aggie, *and that's the business of throwing spitballs.*

17 – NEW FRIENDSHIPS

Miss Fern summoned Aggie and told her Mrs. Primrose wanted her to come to the main office. Aggie liked the offices in the Main Building. Everything smelled of polished wood, and the tall windows were framed by brocade draperies. Some rooms emitted the muffled tones of musical instruments during practice hours. Aggie kept her violin in a closet in one room and practiced three times a week. When her hour of practice was up, Mrs. Primrose always knocked on the door to tell her. Now, Aggie was curious as she knocked on the big cherry-wood door to Mrs. Primrose's office.

Mrs. Primrose opened the door and invited Aggie to come in and sit down in one of the upholstered mahogany chairs. Mrs. Primrose sat opposite Aggie, folded her hands on the desk, and studied her a moment through rimless glasses that slanted up at the lower corners. Mrs. Primrose had a grey topknot, and a chain connected to her glasses to keep them in place in case they fell off her nose. She wore a creamy blouse under a heather-brown suit. To Aggie, Mrs. Primrose looked elegant. She smiled at Aggie and then began the subject on her mind.

"Well, Agatha, I understand you are enjoying school."

"Yes, Mrs. Primrose."

"There's a possibility that you could skip a grade."

"There is??" Aggie thought about that and how it was when she skipped a grade in the city: how the teachers didn't explain the rules of the games played in class; how she already knew how to read and count when she started school; and how the first-grade teacher put her to work teaching reading to a small group of students. Finally, the teacher recommended she skip a grade. But she skipped into a class where they played a new game she had never seen before – a game called "flash cards." What was that teacher doing with those big cards called "flash cards?" Everyone took a turn standing and giving answers; but the teacher didn't explain how to play. The teacher was tired and impatient. It wasn't until Aggie came to the children's home that she figured out what those cards were. She also figured out addition and subtraction. Then she discovered division because the teacher made it fun. She broke out of her reverie,

"Gee, Mrs. Primrose, I-I don't know – "

"I understand, Agatha. You have good friends in the grade you are now attending. With all the changes in your life during the past few years, and what I know about your school record in the city, another change might be one too many??"

"Well – something like that."

"Would you like to stay with your friends in fifth grade?"

"Yes, Mrs. Primrose."

"Yes. Yes, I thought that might be your decision. It was the decision I would have made, but I wanted to be sure you were of the same mind. Now, there's something else. You have been invited to dinner at the home of one of your friends tomorrow night. Take your violin along. They'll come by for you tomorrow night at 5:30. Oh, and Agatha – Miss Fern tells me you have written some music. Take that along, too. You will have a good time. That's all for now, dear." Mrs. Primrose stood, and accompanied Aggie to the door.

"Thank you, Mrs. Primrose." Aggie left the office to the muffled sounds of a trumpet somewhere in one of the practice rooms in the building. Out in the sunshine, Aggie was relieved to know she would be with the same friends she had had since third grade. The Huntingtons came by the next evening, and Aggie enjoyed joining in on the repartee between the two boys, Marvin and Bret, with their parents. There was much teasing back and forth. A maid brought each course to the table. And afterward, while Bret and Marvin played ping pong in the next room, Mrs. Huntington sat down at the piano and played accompaniments to Aggie's violin. Then they tried the music Aggie brought along. Mrs. Huntington experimented with accompaniments for each song and, for Aggie, the evening was totally impressive. Before leaving, Mr. Huntington showed Aggie the library and loaned some books to her. The family piled into the car and took her home.

"Thank you for a wonderful evening! And the dinner was so delicious!" Aggie slid out of the car.

"There will be more evenings, Aggie," they told her before she shut the car door.

That night, it seemed there were more than the usual globby cold cream wads, a.k.a. spitballs, dropping on her.

18 – MORE THAN MUSIC LESSONS

Aggie woke up to the thrashing of a feather pillow. She grabbed a corner and covered her head with her other hand.

"Stop! Stop! I'm awake, Bets! I'm going to get even with you! Just you wait!"

"Have fun last night??" Betty yanked the pillow out of Aggie's grip.

"Yeah! It was all fun!"

"I missed you at dinner! But it's your turn to miss me tonight! I'm going to a birthday dinner at a friend's house!"

"Whose party?" Aggie slid out of bed and stretched.

"Gloria Benham's. And my boyfriend, Eddie, will be there." Betty hopped onto her bed, grabbed a hairbrush, and began counting a hundred strokes through her curly hair.

"I'm going to a friend's house next week," Aggie announced.

"Annnd," Bets interjected, "Clair and Marie are going to a birthday party next Saturday. Poor Miss Fern won't have anyone to eat with, if we keep going to things."

In the weeks that followed, Aggie went to the city with the Huntingtons to see a musical and a play. Then, one Saturday afternoon, Mrs. Huntington took Aggie on a walk to a house near the lake. Mrs. Gabelmeister answered the door and a small Scottish terrier leaped out the door, barking.

"Stop that, Ambrose!" Mrs. Gabelmeister scooped the dog up into her arms. "These are friends who have come to see us!" Her accent had a charming edge to it.

"Mrs. Gabelmeister, this is Aggie. She plays the violin," Mrs. Huntington opened the conversation after all were seated in a cozy parlor filled with plants and a grand piano. A softly-hued Oriental rug on the floor appealed to Aggie. And after Ambrose had settled on Mrs. Gabelmeister's right foot, he kept an eye on Aggie. One wall was lined with books, and French doors opened onto a garden. Aggie turned her attention back to Mrs. Gabelmeister.

"My husband and I came to America just before World War I," she informed Aggie. Mrs. Huntington nodded at Aggie, as though she knew about the Gabelmeisters' origins, already. "I play the violin and piano," Mrs. Gabelmeister added.

Aggie was impressed. Here was someone who played two instruments! Aggie loved the violin, and had never really played the piano. Well, what she had really done was play around on the piano, making up her own chords and tunes. Mrs. Gabelmeister stood.

"My teakettle is simmering. Excuse me a moment, please, while I make some mint tea for all of us." She left the room. Mrs. Huntington leaned toward Aggie.

"How would you like to take violin lessons from Mrs.

Gabelmeister?"

"Me?" Aggie's jaw dropped. "Me? Take lessons from Mrs. Gabelmeister? Oooooh, Yes! I'd love to!" Aggie exclaimed in a hoarse whisper. "But do you think I'm good enough? I've only been playing for two years!"

"Why, yes, I think you are ready for private lessons! And the cost will be covered."

"Oh – thank you, Mrs. Huntington! I'll *love* taking lessons, and I'll practice hard!"

Mrs. Gabelmeister became more than a violin teacher. On Saturdays, after Aggie finished her chores at the dorm, she took her violin and headed for her teacher's home. After an hour or two of lessons, Mrs. Gabelmeister often invited Aggie to stay for tea, or help make cookies, then stay for dinner. Then, when it was dark, Mrs. Gabelmeister walked Aggie home and gave her lessons in astronomy on clear nights. When Mr. Gabelmeister was home from his trips to set up his photography exhibits, Aggie learned about photography.

One Saturday morning in spring, after the violin lesson, Mrs. Gabelmeister invited Aggie to help move the plants out to the patio and then stay for lunch. They cleaned off the round metal umbrella table and wiped off the four chairs. After spreading cream cheese on bagels and making mint tea, they sat on the patio and admired the beauty of the budding trees, the flagstones, and the plants set around in groups along the edge of the area. The first robins gave off their territorial chirps, and the sun warmed Aggie and Mrs. Gabelmeister. Mr. Gabelmeister arrived and joined them on the patio.

"I'm having an exhibition at a museum in the city next month," he announced. "I hope you get to see it."

"I do too," Aggie smiled.

"Perhaps you can see it with the Huntingtons," Mrs. Gabelmeister suggested. "We might be able to join you."

"That would be wonderful!" Aggie bubbled with enthusiasm.

Mrs. Gabelmeister leaned across the table and took Aggie's hand. Her eyes danced with excitement.

"But first, we must have more practice time, because I have arranged that my pupils will perform in a recital!"

Aggie gulped. *Perform on the violin in front of people? All by myself? It's different, playing in the school orchestra. A recital – wow!*

"Could you come on Wednesdays after school?"

"I think so – I'll make sure. I'll ask Miss Fern and Mrs. Primrose."

"I'm certain it will be all right, as long as you don't have any after-school activities on Wednesdays." Mrs. Gabelmeister released Aggie's hands and sat back in her chair with a look of anticipation and satisfaction. "Let's practice a little more music now, and see if we can find some solos for you to play at the recital." They took their plates and cups to the kitchen and returned to the piano.

Aggie enjoyed playing several kinds of music that she had already been practicing. They chose Shubert's "Serenade" and Handel's "Arioso."

Suddenly, it was late afternoon, and Mrs. Gabelmeister prepared a light supper. Mr. Gabelmeister brought out some of the photographs from his darkroom.

"These are some of the photos I am thinking of hanging in the exhibit," he announced. "I am trying to achieve with light and shadow the same effect the old master painters achieved."

18 – MORE THAN MUSIC LESSONS

Aggie woke up to the thrashing of a feather pillow. She grabbed a corner and covered her head with her other hand.

"Stop! Stop! I'm awake, Bets! I'm going to get even with you! Just you wait!"

"Have fun last night??" Betty yanked the pillow out of Aggie's grip.

"Yeah! It was all fun!"

"I missed you at dinner! But it's your turn to miss me tonight! I'm going to a birthday dinner at a friend's house!"

"Whose party?" Aggie slid out of bed and stretched.

"Gloria Benham's. And my boyfriend, Eddie, will be there." Betty hopped onto her bed, grabbed a hairbrush, and began counting a hundred strokes through her curly hair.

"I'm going to a friend's house next week," Aggie announced.

"Annnd," Bets interjected, "Clair and Marie are going to a birthday party next Saturday. Poor Miss Fern won't have anyone to eat with, if we keep going to things."

In the weeks that followed, Aggie went to the city with the Huntingtons to see a musical and a play. Then, one Saturday afternoon, Mrs. Huntington took Aggie on a walk to a house near the lake. Mrs. Gabelmeister answered the door and a small Scottish terrier leaped out the door, barking.

"Stop that, Ambrose!" Mrs. Gabelmeister scooped the dog up into her arms. "These are friends who have come to see us!" Her accent had a charming edge to it.

"Mrs. Gabelmeister, this is Aggie. She plays the violin," Mrs. Huntington opened the conversation after all were seated in a cozy parlor filled with plants and a grand piano. A softly-hued Oriental rug on the floor appealed to Aggie. And after Ambrose had settled on Mrs. Gabelmeister's right foot, he kept an eye on Aggie. One wall was lined with books, and French doors opened onto a garden. Aggie turned her attention back to Mrs. Gabelmeister.

"My husband and I came to America just before World War I," she informed Aggie. Mrs. Huntington nodded at Aggie, as though she knew about the Gabelmeisters' origins, already. "I play the violin and piano," Mrs. Gabelmeister added.

Aggie was impressed. Here was someone who played two instruments! Aggie loved the violin, and had never really played the piano. Well, what she had really done was play around on the piano, making up her own chords and tunes. Mrs. Gabelmeister stood.

"My teakettle is simmering. Excuse me a moment, please, while I make some mint tea for all of us." She left the room. Mrs. Huntington leaned toward Aggie.

"How would you like to take violin lessons from Mrs.

"You are doing just that," Mrs. Gabelmeister assessed. "And, Aggie, it's what you must work on in your music. The louds and softs in music are like light and shadow. It makes the contrasts with notes that Mr. Gabelmeister does with light. It creates a response, either with a view of art or a listener to music."

Aggie felt the day had been rich as she left to go home. But the day wasn't over. Mrs. Gabelmeister threw a shawl around her shoulders while Aggie shrugged into her jacket. Out on the sidewalk, Mrs. Gabelmeister grabbed Aggie's arm.

"Look, Aggie! See above you? Remember where the Big Dipper was last fall? And remember how we noticed changes in the constellations this winter?"

"Yes, I remember," Aggie responded as she let her head fall back for a look at the sky.

"Now, what do you see?"

"Oh – there's the Big Dipper, over there!"

"And there's Orion and his dog – and see Orion's belt?" It stretched Aggie's imagination, but she saw all of it. *She is helping me to see everything.*

Back at the dorm, Miss Fern asked Aggie if she had had a good day. Aggie told her about every learning experience and what a good teacher Mrs. Gabelmeister was. And she added that she learned from Mr. Gabelmeister too.

"It's so exciting, Miss Fern. They know so many things. And the Huntingtons are like that, too."

"It's good you can learn from these fine people, Aggie. And, as I've told all of you girls before, *you can learn as you grow, and when you are grown up, never stop learning. You can be whatever you want to be.*"

19 – MORE LESSONS AND HOWLS

The extra Wednesday lessons helped Aggie improve on technique, even though Ambrose often howled on the high notes. Both Aggie and Mrs. Gabelmeister laughed when that happened and Mrs. Gabelmeister explained that dogs' ears were often sensitive to sounds humans couldn't even hear. Sometimes Mrs. Gabelmeister scooped Ambrose into her arms and she carried him out to the patio and shut the doors.

"Now, my dear, while I have enjoyed accompanying you on the piano, I have chosen one of my piano students to accompany you at the recital. Her name is Miriam Winfield. I believe you know her."

"Yes, yes! She's a friend of mine and we're in the same class at school!"

"When I asked Miriam about accompanying you, Aggie, she seemed just as happy as you are," Mrs. Gabelmeister beamed, and her eyes turned up in an elfin way at the corners. "Of course, Miriam will play some solos, too. I'll invite her over next Saturday, and you can practice together."

That Saturday was the beginning of a good friendship. It also turned out, as usual, to be more than music lessons. Miriam and Aggie looked forward to the recital. Aggie forgot she had had any apprehensions about playing solo in public. Ambrose didn't even howl when they practiced together.

For Aggie, the recital evening cemented her determination to continue playing the instrument she had loved since pre-school days. Miriam played her solos faultlessly, and her accompaniment was perfect. Mrs. Gabelmeister beamed her approval. The program included voice solos, including one by Louise who was taking voice lessons from a friend of Mrs. Gabelmeister.

One afternoon after school, Miriam caught up with Aggie who was heading home for violin practice.

"Aggie, how about coming to junior church choir practice after supper Thursday? Louise sings in it, and so do I. And I know you like singing, because I've heard you and Bets singing duets. Kids from class will be there, so you certainly won't be a stranger."

"Gee, that would be great. I think Bets might like to come, too."

Seeing some of the same kids from her grade outside the classroom put a whole new light on who some of her classmates were when they weren't sitting in a desk across the room. Reverend Butler and Mrs. Butler sometimes arranged extra activities. One Saturday afternoon, everyone met for a beach party that lasted 'til dark when ghost stories were told around a bonfire. Another evening after practice, there was a fudge party. And movies in the social hall.

Then, one evening, kids gathered outside and whispered

about a haunted house.

"Let's go see if it's really haunted," Louise suggested.

"Oh, we know it's haunted," Eddie added with a shiver.

"We can hear moans and groans coming from the second floor when we go home at night."

"Sounds thrilling! Let's go investigate! Lead the way!" Aggie and Bets headed down the walk behind Eddie and Bob, Louise and Miriam. Another boy named Brent caught up, out of breath. A few blocks later, they came upon a neglected-looking frame house with a wrap-around porch. It sat next to a vacant lot near a corner. Twilight revealed dirty windows with no sign of life inside. The group grew silent. No giggling or joking now that they crept quietly up the two steps to the porch and toward the frame door with a frosted window. Eddie tested the knob. It turned. Everyone was quietly surprised. Bunched tightly together, the gang moved through the door to a wide hallway, then to the left, to a parlor, then through to a dining room where plates of a partially-eaten meal still sat on the table. The food had fossilized. The chairs were pushed back from the table. Old newspapers from about ten years before had yellowed beside the plates.

"Looks as though they left in a hurry," Aggie whispered.

"Shhhh!" Bets warned her. In the kitchen, pans stood by the sink. A box of Ivory flakes stood on the shelf above the sink. Rinso laundry soap stood on the shelf next to the Ivory. The kitchen table stood in disarray, as though waiting for someone to clean up after dinner. Back in the hallway, everyone glanced up the stairs to the second floor, but no one decided to go up. Instead, the group moved toward what they expected was another parlor or a bedroom.

A blood-curdling, hair-curling "ooooOOOOooooo" came from the second floor. Someone screamed. Miriam let out a shriek. Everyone scrambled for the door, and a few who couldn't get out fast enough used the parlor window onto the porch. Out on the sidewalk, pale faces glanced up at the second floor windows.

"There! Did you see that?" Brent pointed at an upstairs window.

"No," Eddie stated. "What did you see?"

"Something moved up there!"

"Hey! Just a darn minute! We're missing some people!" Louise exclaimed. Just then, thundering noises descended the hall stairs. The front door was still standing open, and giggles punctuated the silence. Shirley and Claire danced out onto the porch.

"We make good ghosts, don't we?" Shirley laughed. "Hey, Claire, close the door after you! We don't want any spooks to escape!"

"You were all concentrating so hard, we knew you'd never notice if we disappeared," Claire explained.

"You two should spend the night in there!" Bob grumbled. The rest agreed. The group broke up and everyone went their separate ways.

"Yeah, but Miss Fern would notice your absence," Bets spoke up as an afterthought.

"And there wouldn't be so many spitballs on the ceiling, either!" Aggie hiccuped, still recovering from the scare. "But I wonder why the people who lived there left in such a hurry."

"Maybe the ghosts chased 'em out," Louise grinned, and let out an "ooooOOOOOoooo!" to cap off the adventure.

20 – LET'S RUN AWAY

A sunny afternoon. Quiet. Only the birds were chirping, the flies were buzzing, bees were humming, and a soft breeze ruffled Bets' and Aggie's hair. They sat on the steps leading from the French doors at the side of the dorm. The peonies alongside the steps were beginning to bloom. At one end of the girls' dorm, the little girls were napping. At the other end, the older girls were doing homework. Bets and Aggie had finished their homework and sat outside enjoying the warm afternoon. Bets was writing a letter. Aggie was drawing.

"Aggie?"
"Yeah?"
"Let's run away."
"Why? I like it here."
"I don't mean REALLY run away. Just run away a little ways down the sidewalk outside the bushes so we can see how it feels."

"You know how it would feel. Like running down the sidewalk. And then what? Come back to the steps and do what we're doing?"

"Well – sure. Only we'd have that feeling of excitement from running away."

"Oh. You mean that funny feeling when you think you're going to fall?"

"Something like that."

"I know. In science class, the teacher called it adrenalin. But why do you want adrenalin excitement this afternoon?"

"Just to put it to the test. C'mon. Whaddaya say?"

"Did you get some adrenalin excitement when you had poison ivy?"

"No. But – "

"Gee, Bets, I don't need any extra adrenalin this afternoon. I just want to finish this drawing."

"Aw, c'mon, Ag, I don't want to do this alone!"

"Why not? I'll sit here and draw; you can run away and come back, and have your dose of adrenalin."

"How about if we just run down the sidewalk as far as that sidewalk that crosses the campus?"

"Well-l-l-l, as long as that's as far as we go." Aggie put her colored pencils and paper down. "And we can run along that walk that crosses the campus, and come back to what we're doing here on the steps!"

"OK!" Bets put her letter down on the steps. "Ready?"

"Yep." They headed down the walk to the opening in the honeysuckle bushes. The walk joined the one that passed by just outside the bushes. Out they went, and turned to the right to head for the other walk that crossed the campus. But just as they turned, a voice startled them.

"Just where do you girls think you're going?" It was Miss Fern.

"Just down to that walk that crosses the campus," Bets exclaimed.

"Why?"

"Just for exercise," Aggie explained. "See? We left our paper and pencils on the steps, so we could come back." Aggie felt the adrenalin rising.

"Are you sure you weren't running away?"

"Gee, Miss Fern, we wouldn't want to do that!" Aggie protested.

"Then go back to the steps. Or maybe you should go into the dorm."

"Oh, please, Miss Fern," Bets begged, "It's so nice out here. Can't we stay on the steps?"

"You may. But just don't try running outside the bushes. This isn't a school day. I'll be inside, and not very far away!" Aggie and Bets went back to the steps.

"Did you get your dose of adrenalin?" Aggie asked Bets.

"I got it when Miss Fern surprised us," Bets giggled.

"Me, too," Aggie grinned. "But I wonder how she knew what we were going to do. She reminds me of my mother. She had eyes on all sides of her head. Ears, too."

21 – AGAIN, IT'S ALL IN YOUR HEAD

"Miss Conrad, I have an ache in my jaw," Aggie informed her. She pointed to where the ache was. Miss Conrad placed her fingers on the spot.

"There doesn't seem to be anything to complain about. Let's look at your throat." Miss Conrad used a small flashlight to look at Aggie's throat. "I think it's all in your head. You're supposed to see the eye doctor this afternoon, aren't you?"

"Yes. With Marie, Shirley, and Claire."

"Then get a move on. It's a long drive. You're all right."

The drive was a long one, but it was made shorter with all the fun and talk. Miss Wood did the driving. Leaves of many colors were falling, and a wind teased the leaves across the road. The sunlight and bright blue sky peeked through the branches of elm and oak trees. Soon, they came to the town where the eye doctor had his office.

It seemed like a long afternoon in the eye doctor's office. Everyone sat around waiting for their pupils to dilate. Then, after the eye exam, everyone sat around waiting for their pupils to return to normal. But there was plenty of quiet chatter, and the girls enjoyed watching strangers come and go. Aggie still felt a pinchy feeling in her jaw by her right ear lobe. Shirley said she had a pinchy feeling in her left jaw.

"Well, it's probably nothing, Shirley," Aggie tried to reassure her. "Miss Conrad said so. She did tell me it's all in my head, but it feels like it's in my neck."

"Maybe it's the weather," Shirley suggested.

"Yeah, maybe. Like people who get aches in their bones before it rains?" Aggie pondered.

"Sure. That makes sense." Shirley nodded in reply.

"It's time to go, girls," Miss Wood announced quietly. "Do you have everything you came with? Hats, scarves?"

They trooped out of the office and enjoyed the late afternoon ride back.

In the morning, Aggie knew something was different. She felt tight on one side of her neck. She touched the tight side and felt a big swelling.

"Miss Fern? Do I have swollen glands?" Aggie ran her hand over her neck as she approached Miss Fern before breakfast.

"Oh, my, Aggie, I think you might have mumps. I already sent Shirley down to the clinic! You better go down, too, and see what Miss Conrad says!" Miss Conrad said,

"I suppose you exposed the whole town! Well, come along, you can share a room with Shirley."

As they walked toward the room she would share, Aggie thought, *I suppose she's this way because she runs this clinic practically all by herself, unless things get out of hand. No wonder she doesn't smile much. And when she says 'it's all in your head,' she probably hopes it is.*

Aggie grinned, thinking about how everyone stands in line for cod liver oil, and how everyone automatically gags and swallows because it's not a flavor anyone wants to roll around on the tongue to make the moment last. And how, all that gap-and-swallow routine gave the kids a surprise one afternoon, when they walked out the clinic door, realizing they had just swallowed green soap. And Miss Conrad called everyone back to see if they felt all right. Of course, everyone did feel all right. Everyone was so healthy. Probably from all that cod liver oil. But Aggie realized later that they all had missed a great opportunity to cause alarm by faking "not feeling so good."

And that's another thing, Aggie thought, as Miss Conrad paused at the linen closet to get supplies, on their way, *the clinic is pretty much empty most of the time because we're all so healthy. And when it does fill up, it's because of some contagious thing, like measles, mumps, chicken pox –*

"What are you grinning about?!" Miss Conrad snapped.

"Oh, nothing really. Mostly thinking about things I've learned this week." Aggie got into the hospital gown and climbed into bed. She was certain Miss Conrad wasn't as cranky as she appeared to be. Then she remembered something Miss Fern had said, about how things are not always what they seem to be. Sometimes, you just can't tell about something or someone at first glance.

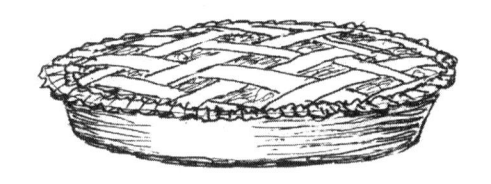

22 – IMMORTAL YOUTH

Math class held Aggie's attention so well, she hardly felt the light tapping on her right shoulder. She turned to see a hand waggling a piece of scrunched-up paper. Aggie pretended to brush off her shoulder as she took the wad. While Miss Burns wrote figures on the board, she quickly opened the paper. It was a note from Amelia, several seats back.

"Meet me outside the back door after school," it read, signed, "Amelia."

Sounds mysterious, thought Aggie, as she pocketed the note. *But it's always interesting and fun with Amelia.* She recalled how Amelia made two perfect apple pies last year in home ec. The pies didn't run all over the oven the way the others did. And the insides were pink instead of yellow. Everyone was anxious to try a piece of Amelia's pie but everyone had to wait 'til lunch when the faculty filed in for the annual home ec. luncheon, so the girls could show off what they had been learning all year. When it was time to cut the pies, girls snagged small bites and discovered Amelia's secret: she had mistaken the salt canister for sugar. A wild scramble followed, as girls quickly cut smaller pieces of the less-perfect pies so there would be enough to go around. But that thought carried Aggie's free-association reverie to the time she and Marie teamed up to make chocolate pudding. They burned the pudding, so – to cover up the taste of burned pudding – they kept adding vanilla. It was the one time that vanilla failed them.

And they made white sauce good enough for bouncing before Mrs. Payne showed them how to thin it down with more milk.

Aggie wandered farther down the trail of memory where she came around a corner to the year before the chocolate pudding, pie, and white sauce. It was the year Mrs. Payne taught sewing, knitting, and crocheting. The big project for Christmas was crocheted potholders. Aggie planned to give hers to Miss Fern. The problem was, Aggie kept adding a stitch at the end of each row and she ended up with what looked like palm fronds and her potholder looked like a palm tree. So she mounted the palm tree on stiff paper, and painted an ocean in the background.

Miss Fern doesn't need a potholder anyway, Aggie had rationalized. The bell rang, which brought Aggie back to the present. Miss Burns raised her voice above the scramble of scraping feet, pencils dropping, and desk lids closing, to give the homework assignment. Aggie wrote it down.

She hurried to the cloakroom, wriggled into her snow pants, pulled her boots on, shrugged into her heavy coat, hurriedly tugged on her mittens, and clamped her fuzzy cap onto her head and over her ears. Then she grabbed her homework assignment and hurried out the door to meet Amelia.

"Several of us are forming an Adventure Club," Amelia explained through puffs of breath that froze on the air. "We're all going to have an initiation together," she went on as they hurried down the walk and crossed the street. They arrived at the ravine where Aggie first discovered the little stream that wound its way to the lake. She found a dry spot on the ground where snow hadn't landed, and placed her notebook there.

Joanne, Marie, Shirley, and Gertrude had just arrived. Everyone looked at Amelia who had obviously come up with the idea.

"See that icy path going downhill?" She pointed. Everyone looked. It certainly was icy. It shot straight toward trees, then shot off to the right toward more trees, but veered off again. It was a treacherous-looking, icy path down to the frozen stream. Amelia continued,

"Each of us will sit down and slide downhill to the stream without touching or grabbing any trees or brush. You can't use your hands. If you succeed, you become a member of the Adventure Club." A buzz of surprise circled among the girls.

Aggie thought, *My dentist says I have good teeth, Miss Fern says I have a good brain. What's going to happen when I explain – toothlessly – how I got a skull fracture?*

Amelia volunteered to go first. She made it all the way to the bottom without touching or grabbing anything. She stood up with a grin of triumph. Shirley said she thought she had the hang of it, so she went next. Then, Aggie sat down and let go. Trees rushed at her, but she leaned and found herself heading away from that cluster of trees to the next. Adrenalin rose inside her, but she found she could stay on the path and avoid the trees. She felt a sense of excitement as she wound on down to the bottom and stood up.

"Gee, that was fun! Let's do it again," she shouted. All the girls took their turns and then started over. The Adventure Club was formally installed. All agreed it would be great to find a new adventure each week, and give it the test.

Everyone went their separate ways, home to dinner. When Aggie got home, she hurried to the bathroom, quickly removed her snow pants and clawed bits of ice off the seat. Marie and Shirley were already wiping ice water off the floor.

"AFTER the adventure is about as much of an adventure as the Adventure," Shirley laughed. Marie nodded in agreement while she washed her face and combed her hair.

Aggie's nose was red from the cold. *If my nose is all that I have to show for it, that's good! None of us broke anything! Except for, maybe, the record for an adrenalin rush.*

23 – GREENER GRASS

Mrs. Pace was helping students rearrange desks, an activity that Aggie liked. Part of the year, she arranged desks in small circles; another part of the year, she had two desks facing each other. Aggie and Joanne had enjoyed working that way. This day, they asked Mrs. Pace if they could continue together in the new arrangement which promised to be four desks per grouping. They happily grouped with Marvin and Adrian.

"Here's an invitation, Aggie," Joanne smiled as she handed a note to her. "It's for dinner at my house Friday night. I hope you can come."

"I do, too! I'll get an OK from Miss Fern as soon as I get home," Aggie promised.

The students hurriedly finished grouping their desks and then Mrs. Pace announced,

"Class, now that you are all in your new groups, I think

you will enjoy working together on a history and geography project." She began writing on the board. "Group One will work on Scotland and England. Group Two will work on Ireland and Wales. Group Three will work on Syria and Mesopotamia. Group Four will work on France and Spain; Group Five, Scandinavia; and Group Six will have Germany and Austria." She turned to the class.

"You may choose any period of time that seems outstanding for your countries, and use any materials you might need for construction of maps or buildings. There will also be a written report to go with this project."

All heads bent toward each other and much planning made the morning go much too quickly. The projects promised to be exciting. Joanne and Aggie had already discovered that fifth grade boys could be funny, so they knew this project was going to be extra fun.

After lunch, Aggie told Joanne she had permission to come to dinner Friday night.

"Goodie, goodie! We'll have fun! We have lots to talk about! And we might even get something done on our project!" Marvin and Adrian sat down at their desks, waiting for Joanne and Aggie to ask why their arms were laden with oatmeal boxes, which, in their minds, had already become the towers in their Scottish castle. The next problem was the moat, which was heatedly discussed 'til it was time for music, and math for the rest of the afternoon.

Friday afternoon after school, everyone gathered in a circle in the gym for ballroom dancing classes. Aggie could hardly wait to go to Joanne's house. She learned the waltz and the box step with Marvin. Each time the teacher announced that it was time to switch, a scramble ensued. Aggie thought what a contrast the scramble was compared to the waltz. Then, 5 o'clock came.

"C'mon, Aggie, it's time to go. My dad is waiting outside," Joanne bubbled. "I'm hungry! Are you?"

"Didn't you hear something growling during the dancing?" Aggie giggled. "I think I scared Marvin!" In the car, after Joanne introduced her dad, the girls fell to chattering about the week and all the homework. Then Joanne said,

"You and Marie started to tell me about the neat ruffled pillows you all have! Tell me more!"

"Oh, I forgot we didn't finish that!" Aggie gazed off into space momentarily. "Well, they're round, flat pillows with ruffles around the edges. They're for decoration on our beds. But we found they sail through the air in a wonderful way! After lights out and all is quiet, we hurl them across the room! We try to be quiet because we don't want to get in trouble, but it's exciting how far they can go. Bets and I tiptoed across the hall and threw ours across the room where all the other girls are sleeping. You know – Shirley, Pat, Marie – "

"Yeah, yeah, go on – "

"Well, one night last week, one of our pillows hit a window shade, and the shade flew up and rattled around and around, making an awful racket! We all dove under our covers and pretended to be asleep. Miss Fern came and checked on us after all that noise, but we were pretty quiet by then. I tried so hard not to laugh, I almost choked! Then Bets let out a snort of giggles under her covers, and after that, she started hiccuping. Those pillows have caused more excitement than Miss Fern knows. At least, I THINK she doesn't know!"

"You might be surprised," Joanne commented. As they chattered, Aggie noticed the winding road Joanne's dad had taken, and the quaint stone bridge that spanned a creek that no doubt ran to the lake. The quaking aspens caught and held the last rays of the sun in their constantly-moving leaves. Gas-powered street lights turned on. Soon, they turned off the main road and took another winding route through birches that gave a feathery effect in the dusk. They parked in the garage of a pleasant-looking two-story brick home with white trim around the high windows, and a fanlight over the double front door.

Joanne's mom greeted them, and Joanne introduced Aggie.

"I'm so glad to meet you, Aggie. I can imagine, after a full day of school as well as dancing until 5:00, that you girls must be ready for dinner. It should be ready soon. Joanne, would you take Aggie's coat? Feel free to look around, and to go upstairs," she smiled.

"Come with me," Joanne invited. They walked through the formal dining room filled with elegant furnishings, and continued on to the spacious living room with many high windows graced by brocade draperies. Aggie became aware that her feet sank into the carpet in a most comfortable way. The furniture reminded Aggie of a style she had seen in a decorating book. Something French. It felt good to sink down into the long couch with its many cushions.

They moved on to the sunroom off one end of the living room. French doors revealed an expanse of lawn and gardens that ended at a cliff's edge overlooking the lake.

How romantic! Aggie thought. Joanne grabbed her arm.

"C'mon up to my room," she invited. They ran up a carpeted, winding staircase to a plushly carpeted hallway with brass wall sconces, and wallpaper in tasteful greens and creams. Joanne led the way down the hallway to a room near the end of the hall. She swung the door open into a room with many windows overlooking the lake. It was a room that could wrap one in coziness, with a chintz bedspread, chintz window treatment, and deep carpeting in which to lose all ten toes.

"Ooooh, Jo! Do you ever hear the lake up here?"

"In summer, on warm nights, I love to have the windows open and listen to the lake as I go to sleep." She fell onto the bed.

Then she sat up on the edge and swung her feet. She brushed her long, dark hair back from her face and gave her bangs a swipe. Her face took on a serious look as she concentrated on Aggie.

"I've been down in the neighborhood where you live, Ag. You know – when I've visited friends. And I notice you have all kinds of playground stuff. And I've heard about your softball games, your Christmases, and all the fun you have in the dorm."

"Uh-huh – " Aggie replied, wondering where this was all going.

Joanne traced the floral pattern on her bedspread, and swung her legs back and forth before she searched Aggie's face. Then she asked,

"Well, tell me, Ag. How do you get in?"

24 – BEFORE TRAINING BRAS

The weather for shorts and halters had arrived. The girls shed their wooly cocoons of winter clothing and donned the bright butterfly colors of summer. Most of the older girls realized they were beginning to fill their halters a little more than they did the summer before. But Aggie was a little slower at it.

One day, Miss Fern came to Aggie's and Betty's room, and to the room across the hall to present the most beautiful symbols of approaching womanhood to Betty, Claire, Shirley, Pat, and Rosie. She gave them satin bras of delicate peach and pristine white. Aggie was dazzled and wondered if she would be forever skinny, as she looked down at the two knobs on her chest – knobs that barely made a difference under her blouse. Of course, her pals ooohed and aaahed as they quickly put on their new glamour garb, and then put the rest of their new treasures in their drawers while Aggie looked on wistfully. She realized that her friends seemed so grown up.

Miss Fern must have sensed Aggie's wish to "catch up" with her peers because, not long after that event, she took Aggie downtown. They stopped at the library where Aggie needed to return some books and check out more.

"I'll be back soon, wait for me," Miss Fern told Aggie. Aggie checked out her books, and then wandered through the rest of the library while she waited for Miss Fern. She found a round table positioned in the afternoon light and started reading one of her books. A quiet voice startled her.

"I'm back," Miss Fern whispered. "Ready to go home?"

"Sure," Aggie closed the book. Back at the dorm, Aggie changed into play clothes to join her friends on the playground. While she put her other clothes away, she became aware of Miss Fern's sewing machine whirring away. Then footsteps came down the hall to the bedroom where Aggie was busy tying her shoes. Miss Fern stood in front of Aggie and presented her with a surprise: two new satin bras, one a delicate peach and the other, pristine white.

"Now let me show you something, Aggie," Miss Fern called attention to some stitching. "As you grow, you can pull these threads and you'll have more room!" Aggie looked closely where Miss Fern was pointing and noticed the loose sewing machine stitches that made the cups smaller so they would fit Aggie. Actually, there were two lines of loose stitching on both cups, to allow for gradual growing.

"What a good idea!" Aggie exclaimed. She looked up at Miss Fern and thanked her for this total surprise. Miss Fern's broad smile and dancing eyes far outweighed anything Aggie could say to express her appreciation. All she could do was say, "Thank you a lot!"

Miss Fern had helped Aggie "catch up" with her buddies. While Aggie put on her new acquisition, she pondered what a difference an article of clothing can make: one little wisp of satin that signals womanhood on the threshold – a change from chrysalis to butterfly. Aggie buttoned her blouse and ran out the door to the playground to join in the softball game.

25 – AGGIE'S MOM

"I don't know which one I like best – Wendell or Marvin," Aggie confessed while brushing her teeth after lunch. Bets stood at the mirror and combed her hair.

"Well, Ag, you really don't have to make up your mind. You can like them both, or even have several boyfriends." Bets put her comb away. "Besides, ballroom dancing starts next week, and you can dance with all of them. Ready to head back to school?"

Aggie put her toothbrush away and rinsed her face. She grabbed a towel and dried her face.

"Yeah, Bets. If they'll dance with me. I feel so awkward and clunky sometimes! Remember when Louise tried to teach me tap dancing? She saw how much fun I had twirling around on roller skates, so she thought I could tap dance. She got so fussed and disgusted that she gave up."

Bets smiled. "Don't worry. Ballroom dancing is different from tap dancing. And someday, your feet might catch up to your hands. C'mon. We'll be late." Bets grabbed Aggie's arm.

"Huh? I don't see – "

"Oh, you know what I mean, Ag. All the fun we have using our hands? You'll have a good time." They fished sweaters out of their lockers. The phone rang. Miss Fern hurried to answer it.

"C'mon, Bets. I'm ready," Aggie prompted.

"Wait, Aggie." Miss Fern had hung up the phone. "You won't be going to class this afternoon. Miss Wood wants you to come to her office. And take your good coat with you."

"What does she want?"

"She'll tell you all about it at her office. I didn't have time to hear all about it because she wanted to catch you before you went back to school. Now both of you hurry."

Betty and Aggie hurried down the stairs and out the door into the warm May sunshine and the smell of lilacs. The honeysuckle bushes were leafing out. The girls parted at the Administration Building, and Betty hurried on to school. Aggie, filled with curiosity and a little apprehension, entered the big French doors. What could be so important that Miss Wood was keeping her out of school for an afternoon??

"Come in, Aggie, take a chair." Miss Wood didn't look up as she invited her into the office. "I'll be ready in a minute." She shuffled some papers together, snapped the edges on the desk, and found a paper clip to hold the papers together. "Now. That's done, and we're ready."

"Ready?"

"We're taking the train to the city to your mother's funeral."

"Mom's FUNERAL??" Aggie stood in disbelief. "I've wondered where she was and had so many questions, why didn't anyone tell me she was dying?"

"We didn't know. She had work at a cafeteria – that's when she wrote to you last – and then she got sick and had to quit. We just found out how sick she was only two days ago."

"But I had so many questions to ask her! Why didn't someone take me to her before she died so I could see her??" Aggie began to cry, more from anger than the shock of her mother's dying.

"She had TB, Aggie. It's contagious. We didn't want to expose you to that. We better get to the train station."

Miss Wood and Aggie remained silent on the way in to the city. Aggie felt resentment roiling up inside her. It was as though kids didn't count, she felt. Adults had all the information, and they sometimes told the kids some tidbit whenever it was necessary.

Aggie's grandmother was at the funeral home. They all silently approached the casket. Her mother was smaller than she remembered her. Aggie remembered how strong her mother was when she was a little girl, watching her mother make bread, sew dresses, paint pictures, cook pot roast with amazing gravy, or simmer appetizing soup. Aggie had always felt secure with her mother. She recalled shopping with her mother, and learning from her strong sense of ethics. Like the time Aggie saw people sampling grapes at the grocery store, and Aggie thought it was what everybody did, so she started picking grapes for herself. Only her mother made her put them back.

"We pay for what we want to eat, Aggie. Sampling grapes without paying for them is stealing." Suddenly, Aggie's anger turned to grief as she realized that she had actually lost her mother. Her mother was really dead. The tears were uncontrollable. Her throat ached. She found a chair and doubled over with crying. The room was silent. Aggie finally sat up and tried to calm herself. Miss Wood handed her a hanky. A combined feeling of grief and resentment made Aggie's chest hurt.

Suddenly, a man in a black suit stood before the group. He made a few comments about death and mentioned Aggie's mother as though he talked about a stranger. He went through the short ceremony, and that was that. It was time to leave.

Aggie looked at her mother once more. She wanted to touch her, but Miss Wood had cautioned her earlier due to the illness. Her mother's face looked so smooth and serene.

Aggie's grandmother spoke to the funeral director. "These lovely flowers should go to the cemetery for the grave. But we will take a few home in memory of this occasion."

Aggie watched her grandmother remove some gladioli and calla lilies from an arrangement. Aggie didn't want any because she thought her mother should have them at her grave. But her grandmother said she should have some in memory of her mother. Aggie hiccuped from all the crying, but she couldn't talk to her grandmother. The afternoon had been such a shock.

Back on the train, no one talked. At home, Aggie asked Miss Fern for a vase. Miss Fern investigated the hall closet and found one. She trimmed the stems, filled the vase with water, and put the flowers in the vase. They both decided the parlor was the best place for the flowers. Aggie stared at the flowers for awhile, thinking that was all she had left. Aggie still had her dad, but he was in a hospital.

Miss Fern invited Aggie to come to her room for a minute. Aggie followed, and Miss Fern motioned for Aggie to sit in the chair by the desk. Aggie briefly noticed the playground noises outside Miss Fern's window.

"Aggie, I know this was a terrible afternoon for you. I know how you have asked about your mother in the past, and how nobody had any real answers. I'm so sorry you had this jolt and all the grief that goes with it." Miss Fern stood and walked to her bathroom, rinsed a washcloth in cold water, and brought it back to Aggie. Aggie wiped her face, and held the cloth to her eyes. Then she let out a long sigh. Miss Fern took Aggie's hands, washcloth and all, and continued.

"It's always hard to lose your parents, especially when you are still growing. You are becoming quite a young lady, Aggie. And while you have lost your real mother today, I want you to know *from now on, I'll be your mom.*"

26 – ALL THAT SOAP

Miss Fern sat sewing under a big old oak tree one summer morning while all the girls wreaked havoc on the playground with a rowdy softball game, seeing how high one could go on the swing, testing out new feats on the trapeze.

Suddenly, she stood up and called for all the "big girls" to come to her. She packed her sewing in her woven basket, clamped the lid tight and said,

"Miss Parker will watch the younger girls on the playground while you girls and I will try out a new project. Follow me." Full of curiosity, the girls followed Miss Fern into the dorm and up the stairs. They followed her into the parlor.

"Find a place to sit, girls. Today, I'm going to teach you how to darn stockings and to embroider. But first we do the darning and other mending." She passed out stockings with holes in the toes or heels, sometimes both. She then demonstrated the weaving method of darning. After everyone understood how to do darning, Miss Fern handed out needles and darning cotton. With everyone busy at mending, she walked over to the nearby radio, switched it on, and moved the dial to a wondrous drama. Miss Fern introduced the girls to the world of soap opera.

What rapturous delight, what tension! While cliffhanger situations unfolded in everyone's imaginations, aided by the magic of radio, the girls quickly finished darning. During commercials, Miss Fern showed the girls how to do the backstitch to mend a pillowcase seam, as she moved through the group to check each girl's progress. Soon, she passed around embroidery cotton and pieces of material with designs stamped on them.

Each day after that, the girls looked forward to that time of morning when it was time to mend and embroider while they listened to the trials and tribulations, the loves and laughs of soap operas. Miss Fern taught how to make a French knot, cross stitch, blanket stitch, satin stitch, the whole panoply of stitches. As their expertise grew, the girls advanced to fancier projects. Miss Fern produced pillowcases and dresser scarves to adorn with colorful designs. First Betty, Pat, and Claire proudly started on their larger projects; then Shirley, Marie, Esther, Aggie, and Rosie began what they hoped would be things of beauty to keep or give away.

But another fascinating element crept into their activities. They thought the commercials were glamorous. They listened to the reasons for buying Lux soap, Palmolive, Camay, Jergens lotion, Colgate toothpaste, and Pond's Cold Cream. Claire's imagination caught fire: She threw her hair back with

a langorous hand, closed her eyes, and declared,
"She's engaged! She's lovely! She uses Pond's!" Everyone giggled at the drama. Then Esther added,
"And now that she uses Colgate, her teeth are whiter, so she's more popular!" Giggles and sighs followed. Imagination ran rampant with all the possibilities of sweet-smelling soap, soft hands that used the right lotion, the romance of gleaming teeth, and all the rest.

The ardent pursuit of morning soaps continued, each plot on each soap building to a fever pitch, and then came the letdown from the recesses of the radio with "Stay tuned for tomorrow when . . . ," capped off with groans of abject disappointment from each girl.

The desire to reap the results of product usage grew as the summer wore on into fall. Of course, school interrupted the day-to-day radio crises. But still the girls wondered: how could any girl obtain those fragrant and good-tasting, skin-smoothing, glamorizing items? The answer came one day in magazines. By filling out coupons for free samples of Lux, Colgate, lipstick, rouge, and all the other transforming miracles of the day, the Post Office became a cornucopia.

But the real magic occurred at Christmastime. Miss Fern gave each of the older girls a dollar for Christmas shopping. Excitement grew with a festive train ride to a larger town where Christmas lights filled store windows, the frosty air made cheeks and noses red. Miss Fern led her entourage to the Five-and-Dime and turned everyone loose, with the agreement to meet by the front door at a certain time. Dollars went as far as possible as little secrets like candy canes, pens, memo pads, barrettes, combs, and small mirrors ended up at the cash register whenever a girl thought none of her friends could see what she had purchased for gift-giving. Back at the dorm, everyone hid little paper bags full of surprises so no one could possibly guess. After feverish wrapping and tagging, those secret stashes, along with much giggling and anticipation, the girls placed their mysterious little packages under the tree. As each day brought Christmas a little nearer, the pile seemed to hold the tree up.

Soon after, other packages appeared under the tree – packages tagged in Miss Fern's writing for: Shirley, Pat, Betty, Rosie, Claire, Sally, Aggie, Esther, Greta – all the girls in Miss Fern's care. It was hard to wait. Girls shook packages, held them to their ears, poked them, and finally gave up and kept busy with church and school Christmas programs. And, since everyone would spend Christmas in private homes, the breathless time for package opening was Christmas Eve. Miss Fern handed out the assortment. As each package that had been shaken and rattled and poked finally had its wrappings torn off, little intakes of breath filled the room. Each girl discovered a beautiful variety of sophistication from Miss Fern. It was an amazing event to find a full-size bar of Palmolive, a regular-size bottle of Jergens Lotion, a full tube of Colgate toothpaste, and a jar of Pond's Cold Cream! Not samples obtained by coupons but regular-size bits of glamour. These were packages of love from Miss Fern – and long after everything was used up, the beauty of the occasion and what these packages meant would live on in each girl's memory.

27 – GRETA KEEPS A SECRET

The *shree, shree, shree* sound of roller skates on concrete sidewalks pleased Aggie. It meant the snow was gone and spring was on its way. The thoughts of lunch also pleased Aggie. Then, school in the afternoon promised lots of interesting happenings in class and a basketball game after school. Her thoughts and the sound of the roller skates almost drowned out someone's calling.

"Wait for me! Are you deaf?" Greta's voice came closer. Aggie turned to see her running to catch up. Greta was out of breath.

"Sorry! I didn't hear you, my skates are noisy," Aggie apologized.

"Uh – huh, well, that's OK," Greta panted. "I wanted to tell you about my new boyfriend." Greta labored between breaths.

"New boyfriend? That's neat, Greta! Who is he?"

"He just moved here. So you probably don't know him."

"What's his name?" Aggie had slowed her skating so Greta could keep up and not have to talk above the noise.

"His name's Paul. He lives near the lake. He doesn't know where I live. I didn't want him to know I live at the children's home."

"But won't he find out anyway? And why should that make a difference?"

"Well, gee whiz, Aggie! He might not like me then, if he knows. After we get better acquainted, and he really likes me, then maybe I'll tell him! I'm really embarrassed about living here."

"Gosh, Greta, why be embarrassed? There's nothing wrong about it. It's not a reform school or anything like that! Only difference between us and the townies is we don't have parents to take care of us." Aggie pondered a moment. "And even if we do have a parent or parents still living, they're sometimes too sick."

"Don't you get it, Ag? We're not like the townies!"

"I don't feel that way with my friends, though. It just doesn't come up! I have an awful lot of fun with my townie friends. And they elected me secretary in class recently. And in Girl Scouts, it's the same way. Birthday parties with townies are fun too. Once in awhile, when the Huntingtons give me tickets to plays in the city, I invite a townie friend to come along." Silence followed. Greta and Aggie were both deep in thought as they crossed the street to their home.

I wonder what it would be like now. With my dad and mom, still, or with my grandma. I love school here, the fun, the friends, all the great things that wouldn't be happening if I still lived with Dad and Mom, or with Grandma. I love them, but this is better since my mom is gone, and my dad is so sick, and my grandma overworked in that big house. Greta broke the silence.

"You could be right, Ag, but I still feel – different. It's good to point out your own family and your own house. I'm going to keep my secret from Paul!"

"You're right about having your own family and home, Greta. But this is a good thing for us since we can't do anything about what's happened to our families. We're family here, now – and Miss Fern is our mom."

"Well – yeah, since you put it that way. At least we're not homeless. But I'm keeping my secret as long as possible."

In the dining room, they all took their places. Miss Fern smiled as she handed a plate down the line to Aggie. Aggie silently thought, *Thanks, Mom! It's good to be home.*

28 – CHANGES FOR MISS FERN'S CHARGES

"Gee, Bets, I'm going to miss you a LOT!" Aggie sat on the edge of her bed and watched Betty pack.

"I'll write to you, Ag. And you'll be graduating, too, in a couple of years. Here – I'll give you some of my notes. They could come in handy." Betty handed a pile of papers across her bed to Aggie.

"Thanks, pal." Aggie leafed through the papers. "Y'know what, Bets? It's just as well Miss Fern is assigning me to help out at Jefferson House. It's time to switch chores anyway, and I'm glad about Jefferson House."

"Well, no wonder, kiddo. It's like an overgrown doll house." Betty continued concentrating on her packing. She pulled a small bag out of a drawer, studied it, tossed it back and forth from one hand to the other. Then she turned and casually tossed the bag on Aggie's bed.

"Want these?" Marbles rolled out of the bag and onto the quilt. Aggie caught her breath.

"Oh, Bets! Oh, yes!" She jumped up and threw her arms around Betty's neck. Betty gave Ag a big hug – and then they both began to sniffle. Aggie found an old hanky rag she hadn't completely torn into strips for spitballs, and blew her nose. Betty wiped her eyes and said,

"I've been here so long, it's home. It's going to be strange leaving here to live with my dad and his new wife."

"I know you'll be happy, Bets. And just think – you'll be a high school freshman!" Aggie brushed away a stray tear and said, "Sa-a-ay, I know just what I want you to have to remember me by!" She fished through a drawer until she found a small locket and placed it in one of Betty's hands.

"It has a picture of Cary Grant in it because it came that way, but I'll find one of me. Someday you'll want to put a boyfriend's picture in it."

"Thanks, Ag, I'll wear it a lot." Betty placed it in a special pocket of a suitcase. Miss Fern appeared at the door.

"Aggie, Betty, it's time for lunch. And right after lunch, Aggie, Miss Sterling wants to see you at Jefferson House, to get acquainted with the routine."

Betty snapped a suitcase shut, and tossed some loose things into a paper bag. On their way to the dining hall, Aggie said,

"I'll be back to say goodbye after Mrs. Sterling shows me the schedule. It shouldn't take long."

"I'll still be here, Ag. My dad isn't expected 'til late in the afternoon."

Mrs. Sterling led Agatha to a room off the large hall on the second floor of Jefferson House. She stood aside while Aggie passed by and entered the room.

"This is your room, Agatha," Mrs. Sterling explained. Agatha looked around at a small room with a cot, dresser and mirror, a chair, and closet. An east window with many panes let in an ample amount of light. A clock in the form of Felix the Cat hung on a wall. Its eyes moved back and forth, and its tail acted as a pendulum, switching back and forth in time with the ticking seconds.

"Now, Agatha, let me show you the rest of the floor – " she led the way down a hallway. "This is your bath. And the cleaning closet is here." She pointed to a door across from the bath. "Now let's see the children's bath."

Agatha followed Mrs. Sterling to a large room with everything built for small people. Four small sinks with mirrors lined one wall. On the opposite wall, four small toilets sat at a level for small people. A bathtub was raised on a foundation so, as Mrs. Sterling explained, "we won't get sore backs bathing the children."

The bedroom area was also a Lilliputian world with two beds per cubicle, two closets, and chests of drawers with mirrors built into the wall. Agatha stared in amazement at the layout.

Downstairs, they entered a large parlor and playroom where chintz draperies hung on the high windows, including the large bay window that faced out onto a sprawling terrace. Upholstered chairs and a sofa, all covered in chintz, were also built to scale for little people. A large dollhouse dominated one corner of the room. The sides unhooked so little people could stand at the dollhouse and rearrange the interior furniture and dolls.

Mrs. Sterling pulled a piece of paper from her pocket, adjusted her glasses, and explained the schedule to Aggie.

"After you make the beds in the morning, you will go to the main dining hall and be with your friends. On Saturdays, you will scrub the bathroom floor, and put clean sheets on the beds. Then you are free to go back to your dorm and join your friends." Mrs. Sterling showed Aggie the laundry chute.

"Do you have any questions, Agatha?" Aggie couldn't think of anything right away, so Mrs. Sterling dismissed her.

"You may start moving in right away, and start assisting me tomorrow," Mrs. Sterling added as Aggie turned to leave.

"Thank you, Mrs. Sterling," she waved and left, anxious to get back to the dorm to see Bets before she left.

But Bets was gone. There was a note with a promise from Bets that she would write with her new address.

"Her dad came sooner than we expected," Miss Fern explained from the doorway. "I know what close friends you have become, and it's always a sad time to say goodbye. Next year, Claire and Louise from downstairs will be saying goodbye."

Aggie felt a tinge of morose feelings welling up inside. She paused by a chest of drawers in preparation for packing. Miss Fern came into the room and sat down on a bed.

"There have been a lot of changes lately, haven't there?" Miss Fern had a sympathetic look in her eyes. Aggie came over to Miss Fern and threw her arms around her neck. Miss Fern gave Aggie a hug.

"It seems to be a rule of life, Aggie," Miss Fern went on. "Constant change seems to be a rule of life."

29 – MISS FERN'S ANNOUNCEMENT

At Jefferson House, Aggie sorted her clothes and put them in the dresser drawers, hung up dresses and blouses, and put fresh sheets on her cot. She mused about how quickly Bets had gone from the life in the dorm. She thought of all the things they had done together: all the drawing, singing, talking; the times when they shared chores at the dining hall, and how Aggie had enjoyed drinking down the bits of leftover cream in the little pitchers; and the games everyone played while the dishwasher processed the dishes.

"Agatha," Mrs. Sterling broke in on Aggie's reverie, "when you're through putting your things away, I need to go over your daily schedule and procedures."

"OK," Aggie responded, "I'm almost finished." Aggie already felt homesick for Miss Fern – her "mom" – and "mom" to everyone in her care.

Well, I'm a seventh-grader now. Just next year and then on to eighth grade and, after that, high school. I hope I can go to art school after that! Aggie closed the dresser drawers, shut the closet door, and adjusted the rug by the bed. The sun shot rays of warmth and light into the room and made Aggie feel better about the changes.

Well, on to Mrs. Sterling, now – She found Mrs. Sterling in the downstairs parlor where all the little kids were playing.

She could hear their high voices talking and laughing long before she entered the room. Mrs. Sterling sat in one of the two adult wing chairs in the room. She motioned to Aggie to sit in the other chair.

"I will take the children outside soon and then they'll have lunch. After that, it's their nap time." Mrs. Sterling smiled. "May I call you Aggie?"

"Yes, of course," Aggie replied, glad to drop the sober-sounding "Agatha" that Miss Fern used only at serious times when she wanted Aggie's full attention. When things were really serious, or when she had to scold Aggie about something, she often used Aggie's full name, "Agatha Marian Broward," in a stern voice. But most of the time, Aggie saw a loving smile on Miss Fern's face. She had that same loving smile for each girl. Aggie turned to ask a question of Mrs. Sterling who suddenly had a little boy sitting in her lap. He looked so neat and clean, with his freshly washed dark brown hair and starched blue and white playsuit, the kind with buttons around the waist of the blouse so the shorts could be buttoned to the waist. Mrs. Sterling had her arms around the little boy, who busily sucked his thumb and, with the other hand, fondled one of the buttons on his playsuit.

"This is Jeffry. We call him Jeff," Mrs. Sterling said. I think he's getting sleepy. But when he gets outside, he'll play, then we'll have lunch, and he'll sleep well at nap time." Jeff's eyelids were by now at half-mast, as Aggie introduced herself. Mrs. Sterling stood him up, took his hand and announced to all the children that they would go outside for awhile. She turned to Aggie and said,

"I'll need you after supper every night. And tonight is bath night."

"I'll be here," Aggie assured her, and left to go up to the dining hall. *This will work out well,* she thought on her way to lunch. *I'll still get to see friends, have meals with them, and also help with the little kids.*

Evening turned out to be extremely busy. As each child's bath was finished, Aggie grabbed the squirmy, wet body that almost squeaked with cleanliness. She quickly toweled the child off, while Mrs. Sterling worked on bathing the next child. By the time the baths were done, Mrs. Sterling had sudsed and rinsed twelve wriggling bodies and Aggie had toweled down twelve wriggling bodies. While this ritual proceeded, there was much singing and giggling, and running up and down the hallway with nothing on.

Finally, each child had somehow gotten his or her seersucker pajamas on, but a few chubby little fingers couldn't quite manage the buttons. Aggie helped with the buttons while Mrs. Sterling combed everyone's hair into a neat and tidy style. Mrs. Sterling led the children to their beds and heard their prayers while Aggie cleaned up the bath, gathered all the bath towels, and tossed them down the laundry chute. She heard Mrs. Sterling say,

"Goodnight, children," as she closed the door with the

window in it, and twelve little people in twelve little beds fell asleep. Gradually. Almost. Aggie realized that the window in the bedroom door was a great idea. A little whispering, some giggling, scurrying feet, and Mrs. Sterling glanced through the window before she opened the door and settled a lot of pre-sleep restlessness with her authoritative manner. Soon everything was quiet, and Aggie realized her own bedtime had come.

Aggie snuggled into bed and felt sleep creeping up on her as the tail of the cat on the wall swung back and forth, counting the seconds. Then the phone rang. She heard Mrs. Sterling's quick footsteps, and then she heard her voice answer, softly.

"Hello. Yes, Fern. Oh. Of course. In the morning? Yes, I'll tell her right away." The click of the receiver into its cradle ended the conversation. Soft footsteps approached Aggie's room. The footsteps paused outside her door. Then there was a light tapping.

"Aggie?" Mrs. Sterling whispered.

"Ummm – Yes?" Aggie whispered in return.

"Miss Fern wants to see all the girls in the morning before breakfast. So when you're through here, go up to the hall and they'll all meet in the parlor." Mrs. Sterling paused. "Then, of course, you will all go to breakfast."

Aggie struggled up onto her elbows. "Did Miss Fern say what it's about?"

"She'll tell you all about it in the morning, dear. Now, goodnight." The footsteps retreated.

Aggie's mind began to ask questions and fantasize about all the possible reasons for a before-breakfast conclave. *Did someone die? Run away? Or was a long-lost parent found to be a prince or princess, or a millionaire, or who-knows-what, returned to claim a child that had been mothered by Miss Fern for, lo, all these years?*

Stop it! Aggie mentally scolded herself. *Go to sleep, brain!* Aggie stretched, adjusted the blanket, and then recalled other conclaves. Like the time someone had picked all of Greta's prize zinnias and taken them to school. Or the mystery of who pulled up Shirley's young apple tree. Or the complaint that the girls were being scared by the ghost stories Aggie was writing. Or –

Aggie's brain had wound down. All of a sudden, it was morning.

All the girls were gathered in the parlor when Aggie arrived. Miss Fern sat, patiently waiting. As Aggie found a chair and pulled it into the circle, Miss Fern looked down at the floor. Then, she looked up and glanced quickly at each girl as her eyes swept the gathering. She looked down at her hands, cleared her throat, and started in.

"Girls, you have been my family. Now I must return to another family, my mother and father. They are getting on in years, and need help. I want to spend time with them, helping them. I haven't seen them for awhile, and I don't really know how long they will be around." Miss Fern reached into her pocket for a hanky. Someone in the group began to sob and then others began sniffling and sobbing. Tears ran down Aggie's cheeks. Miss Fern removed her glasses and wiped her eyes with her hanky.

"I guess I should have waited until after breakfast to tell you this," Miss Fern continued. She sighed, "But I guess we should wash our faces and go to breakfast. Right, girls?"

As the girls rose to leave the parlor, Miss Fern hugged

each one. Aggie was last in line.

"Aggie, I have a niece just about the same age as you. I hope it will be possible for you to come out and visit." With that little gem of news to hang onto, Aggie replied,

"Me, too." She swallowed hard. *What will it be like without Miss Fern? She's my other mom. When I think how it all began, how I dreaded coming here, how lucky I've been through the years, and now I have hopes of visiting Miss Fern some day. Meanwhile, there's high school ahead. I hope I can continue on with my townie buddies!* Aggie ran to the bathroom to wash her face.

"C'mon, girls," Miss Fern called. "Breakfast!"

Founded On Love

'Twas love that grew the leafy fence
    surrounding them at play;
'Twas love that built the buildings
    to shelter them each day.
'Twas love brought men and women
    to this modest place;
'Twas love that turned the place to home
    and grew a smiling face.

'Twas love that suffered little ones
    to come to Him that day;
'Twas love that helped them find a faith
    with which to find the Way.
'Twas love – *this* love that set a date
    in 1894,
And helped some people kindle it
    and open up a door.

'Twas through this door they came and went –
    the children of His love.
They shall go forth to spread His light
    and grow to heights above.

'Twas love that said,
    "Come unto Me;"
'Tis love that beckons still;
'Tis love that raises "homeless" ones
    to live His holy will.

Poem and illustration by
Corinne Briscoe Elliott,
circa 1957

EPILOGUE

One summer after Aggie's first year in high school with her townie buddies, Miss Fern invited her to come visit and get acquainted with her niece. Aggie and Miss Fern's niece went to summer camp for two weeks and had a wonderful time. Miss Fern applied to adopt Aggie; but those were the years when social workers limited adoption to couples, not single parents. Aggie returned to her high school and graduated.

The years that followed included Aggie's marriage, three children and success for her husband. Aggie also followed her own interests, eventually graduating an art school via correspondence, and also obtaining a college degree, after her children were grown. She enjoyed exhibiting and selling her paintings and note cards, and also achieved considerable fulfillment from her professional writing experiences.

When Aggie and her family took a trip to the area of her childhood, Miss Fern met them. Aggie looked at her "other mom" and thought, *In a way, Miss Fern is meeting her "grandchildren."*

Miss Fern and Aggie kept in touch until Miss Fern's death.

☙❧

ABOUT THE AUTHOR

Corinne Briscoe Elliott always enjoyed sharing her ideas and experiences through the written word, and ultimately obtained a college degree, with high honors, with special concentration in writing. In addition to sharing her own experiences through this book and various articles, she also wrote for newspapers, periodicals, a reference book company, a realtor and a radio station, winning numerous awards for her advertising copy, as well as mention in editions of "Who's Who in American Writers" and "Who's Who in American Women."

She sold her first painting to a police officer in a bar on the south side of Chicago at the age of eight, and went on to earn substantial art credentials and achieve considerable success as a commercial artist and watercolorist, exhibiting and selling her art throughout the United States and gaining a place in "Who's Who in American Artists."

Whether writing, painting, drawing, or crafting her note cards, her vantage point was always positive and sunny, expressing appreciation for the beauty and humanity in her surroundings, and leaving her audience uplifted. Her creative legacy not only edifies and inspires, but warms the heart and encourages all to look on the bright side in all instances.

AFTERWORD

The orphanage at Lake Bluff, Illinois was known by various names throughout its history, starting out as the Methodist Deaconess Orphanage upon its founding in 1894. In 1945, the name of the institution was officially changed to the Lake Bluff Orphanage. In 1955, the Lake Bluff Orphanage was renamed as the Lake Bluff Children's Home, and then as the Lake Bluff-Chicago Homes for Children, in 1969.

By the mid-1950's, foster care for children was shifting increasingly to placement with individual families, and to the development of community-based programs throughout the Chicago area. In 1969, the doors of the Lake Bluff Children's Home were closed forever, marking the end of an era in which so many young lives were much enhanced by caring staff and other contributors to their well-being.

In 1979, the buildings were demolished, and single family residences now occupy the former site of the Children's Home. However, a historical marker, dedicated in November 2010, has been placed in a sidewalk panel at the northeast corner of East Scranton and Evanston Avenues in Lake Bluff, to memorialize the children and staff who lived and worked at the Lake Bluff Children's Home.

In 1986, Lake Bluff-Chicago Homes for Children changed its name to ChildServ, to better reflect the shift from institutional and residential care to multi-faceted community-based programs.

The Lake Bluff History Museum, which has a web presence at www.lakebluffhistory.org, maintains the Lake Bluff Children's Home archives and features a well-researched and beautifully illustrated exhibit about the

Children's Home that includes a photo of the author on her wedding day, at the reception held on the grounds of the institution. For years, she was known only as "the Children's Home bride," since the museum had no way of identifying the people in the photo. In recent years, a chance meeting between a member of the museum board of directors and a cousin of the author brought to light the identity of the newlywed couple in the photo and ultimately lead to a valuable connection between the author's family and the museum.

Also available at the Lake Bluff History Museum is a feature-length documentary film about the history of the Lake Bluff Children's Home: "A Childhood Lost & Found," by Kraig Moreland, which depicts not only the history of the orphanage itself but also its significant effects on the lives of the young people who called it home.

Though time has lead to the obliteration of the buildings, treasured memories of the Lake Bluff Children's Home will live on in the hearts and minds of those who benefited from their years in residence there. It is our hope that the stories told herein will serve to add some color to the images of residents and staff whose influence ripples on vibrantly to this day.

Made in the USA
Charleston, SC
08 September 2011